INTERNET DATING

It's Complicated...
But It Doesn't Have To Be!

LAURA SCHREFFLER

A Guide To Dating
In The Digital Age

Internet Dating 101...It's Complicated, But It Doesn't Have To Be: A Guide To Dating In The Digital Age by Laura Schreffler (aka "Laura Love") is published by New Chapter Press (www.NewChapterMedia.com) and is distributed by the Independent Publishers Group (www.IPGBook.com). All Rights reserved by Laura Schreffler and New Chapter Press.

We encourage readers to also visit www.LauraLoveAdvice. com. Are you having problems with your love life? Do you constantly pester and nag your friends, family and co-workers with your relationship problems? Do you constantly seek advice on what to do, how to handle certain situations? Do you wonder how to how to get your man to commit to you? Or a strategy on how to best get the attention of girl or a guy? WHEN YOUR FRIENDS, FAMILY AND CO-WORKERS ARE SICK OF TALKING TO YOU, LAURA LOVE IS HERE TO HELP! Laura Schreffler is available to give you an assessment of your romance or relationships issue. For a fee of $15 – just a glass of wine in New York City or Los Angeles – you can email Laura a summary of your situation. Laura Love will respond with her sage love advice and give you proper route to go. The $15 fee covers one email response from Laura, plus an additional counter-response. Starting with the third email from Laura, an additional fee of $8 will be charged for each subsequent email. Email your question to NewChapterPress@ gmail.com.

Follow Laura on Twitter at @LauraLoveAdvice and like her LauraLoveAdvice.com fan page on Facebook. You can also read Laura's columns and love advice at www.LoveTrekker. com.

ISBN - 978-1-937559-00-7

Printed In the United States

Contents

INTRODUCTION

"I'm sorry, I can't hang out tonight. I've got a hot date."

This wasn't a shocking revelation from my friend Alexandra, and I was willing to bet that her date a) wouldn't be hot and b) wouldn't last longer than an hour. She's one of those girls who fantasizes that each and every man is "the one" only to realize that her dreams don't match up with reality. Then again, she also scores most of her dates online.

True to form, her latest "love interest" was one of her online finds. Though she had been talking to him for a mere two days before they decided to meet, she was optimistic.

"OKCupid is amazing," she enthused. "I've been talking to the greatest, cutest guy on there. He likes Paris and he wants kids, too. Tonight is going to be a blast!"

"Sounds like you're a match made in heaven," I deadpanned. I was skeptical, as most of the men I've met that appear to be perfect on paper rarely are.

Naturally, Alex didn't call to discuss her date the next day or the day after that. My dear friend has a habit of avoiding thinking about unpleasant things. I get it, I really do. If you never mention something, it's almost as if the incident never existed. She subscribes to the "If a tree falls in the forest and no one is around to hear it, does it make a sound?" school of thought.

"So, how did it go?" I asked her – quite casually – when we met up for coffee a week later.

"How did what go?"

I knew it – avoidance!

Careful not to sound condescending, I reminded her, "Your great date. Was it amazing? What did you do? Where did he take you?"

She raised her eyebrows, made a face and gazed into her coffee cup as if it was a crystal ball and could predict her future (or erase her past).

"He turned out to be crazy," she admitted.

"Crazy how?" I was curious. I had never been out on an online date before, you see.

"Crazy like five feet tall instead of six, had bad breath and tried to suck my face on the way out of the bar even though we had *zero* chemistry. Crazy like when I wouldn't kiss him, he started screaming at me in the middle of the street. I had to call a car service. There was no way I was driving back home with him," she responded.

As an afterthought she added indignantly, "And he made me go Dutch! Can you believe it?"

I made some kind sympathetic tut-tut here-here noise I've heard my grandmother make and remained silent. For the record, I am almost *never* completely quiet. I've been through every sort of cruddy relationship situation you can imagine – and learned life lessons from them all, might I add – but there was nothing I could say to make her feel better about this tale of cyber woe. I was still reeling from the fact that she had gotten into a car with a virtual stranger.

It wasn't like I hadn't heard this story before, though. Like most of us, Alex has a pattern. She would go out with a guy she had started speaking to only days before on OKCupid, Match or eHarmony (she belonged to all three), decide it was her perfect partner after a few hours of chatting, be crestfallen after meeting in person and discovering his real life self wasn't as cool as his online persona and end the date quickly. Stir and repeat. The only thing that ever changed was the guy in question's user name (and even those all blended together after awhile).

How To Lose a Guy in 10 Days? I think not. Alex's life was way more 'How To Lose a Guy in 24 Hours.' Kate Hudson, watch out – you've got competition!

As Alex began to gush about yet *another* potential online love interest, I tuned out and realized that the sound I was hearing wasn't the humming of her voice, but the rusty cogs of my brain slowly turning. I began to think (damn cobwebs made it hard though).

Why do so many smart women become complete idiots when it comes to men? Why would my intelligent, beautiful, city savvy friend potentially risk her life by getting in some dude's car when she didn't even know his full name? Was online dating really like shopping for a partner? Did anyone really and truly have any success looking for love on the Internet? I vowed to find out for myself.

THE NEXT STEPS

But first, I needed to check my Facebook page.

I admit it, I was a huge Facebooker. I was one of those people who left her page up all day and checked to see if anybody had commented on my page from my mobile phone. I was obsessed.

Unfortunately, I was also obsessed with constantly checking my ex's page to see what he was up to. Yeah, sad and pathetic I know. I'm not proud of myself, but I'm not going to apologize for it, either.

I had just broken up with Jake, and, while I was mostly over him, I was still into the bad habit of checking his Facebook page as regularly as I had when we were a couple. However, unlike when we were still together, this voyeuristic peek into his private life was painful.

I quickly clicked off his page after seeing that

he'd befriended a pretty new girl. "Bastard," I thought, as I also silently berated myself for the compulsive need to look at his page. I applied the terms "fool" and "dumbass" to myself, for my failure to suppress the need to check up on him in the first place.

Needing a distraction, I scrolled through my news feed, and saw that an acquaintance had changed her relationship status to "It's complicated." The woman in question was a semi-public figure in her thirties. Sharing her very personal details with friends including moi – a person she'd met twice – didn't seem like a smart or strategic move.

I realized that I didn't *want* to know if her relationship was complicated. If she were having problems with her boyfriend, surely airing her dirty laundry to all 2,063 of her friends wouldn't help the situation any. What would come next? A fluctuating scale of relationship status updates ranging from "Single" to "In a Relationship" and back again until one of her real friends finally told her enough was enough and causing her to delete her account?

Though we weren't *real* friends (as opposed to just Facebook friends), I wanted to tell her to wise up. I wanted to tell Alex to get with the program, too, and avoid getting into cars with men who might by serial killers or rapists. Most of all,

I wanted to yell at *me* and say "Stop checking up on your ex! It's over, and it's just making you unhappy. It's time to get the hell on with your life!"

Poof! There went the last of my cobwebs as an idea began to take shape. I was going to write a book on the ups and downs to looking for, keeping and talking about love online. I would become a champion of the online and social media arenas, like Cupid with a bigger body, longer hair, less nudity and far fewer arrows (I shouldn't be trusted with those things, seriously).

I decided that, not only would I would master the online dating game, but I would teach others to beat it, as well.

Want to know how well I did? Well, let's put it this way: I said sayonara to both my ex *and* his Facebook page, and I have never, ever looked back. On that note, now it's time for *you* to reap the rewards of the lessons I had to learn the hard way.

Virtually Yours,

Laura Schreffler

"Laura Love"

SECTION 1:

ONLINE DATING

PART I:

WHAT'S AVAILABLE ON THE WWW

CHAPTER 1:

AN INTRODUCTION TO DATING SITES

OK, admit it. At one point or another in your life you've thought, "There is no way I will date online. That's for people who can't get dates in real life. I don't have a problem getting dates, therefore I will never, ever in a million years be pathetic enough to sign up for Match.com."

So yeah, about that...sorry, but eventually, you're going to change your mind. Fact. Whether it's because your curiosity bested you, or you just can't seem to meet the right guy in reality or all of your friends are doing it, you *will* try online dating at some point in your life (unless you're already married and plan on staying that way, that is).

Although you swore you'd never do it, here you are. Feeling as shameful and guilty as if you were caught watching porn, you log on to Match.com or PlentyofFish.com to see what the fuss is about. Lo and behold, you realize that you kind of like this looking for love malarkey. You discover that online dating isn't just for dateless dorks like you assumed, but it's a lot like shopping for your perfect mate. As Charlie Sheen might say, "Winning!"

There are roughly 54 million singles in America. Of that number, 5.5 million are online dating. It is now the second most common way of meeting people,[1] just behind being set up through friends.

That means that 1 in 5 singles wind up in a committed relationship with someone they met online these days. While we're talking statistics, 1 in 6 singletons actually *married* someone they met on the Internet – which is *17%* of all Americans.[2] Um, whoa.

So dispel that notion that online dating isn't an organic or natural way to meet a potential partner, wise up and get with the program. This is the natural evolution of modern-day dating. It's a new time, a new age and almost everyone uses the Internet. If they don't, they have a valid excuse – like living in a country without electricity or clean water. That said, I have friends living in the rainforest who use solar power to turn on

• •

1   *Searles, Rebecca.* February 7 2012. <http://www.huffingtonpost.com/2012/02/06/online-dating-common-couples-meet_n_1257243.html>.

2   *Match.com and Chadwick Martin Bailey, 2010, <cp.match.com/cppp/media/CMB_Study.pdf>*

their computers, so really, those of you with easy access to the Internet have absolutely no excuse not to be taking advantage of it.

It's time to think outside the box and stop hating on something you haven't even tried. There are benefits to dating online. For example, if your life is your career, you may not have time to date like a regular human would. You're busy, in demand and either chained to your desk or constantly in and out of boring business meetings. If you live in New York or Los Angeles, you're probably stuck going endless high-profile functions where you'll definitely schmooze, but not in the name of love: there will be nary a straight man in sight. What you're *not* doing: spending your Wednesday nights at a salsa class, or at a quiet local bar or even in a bowling league. No, you're dreaming about when you'll be able to pass out and go to sleep (preferably by 9 p.m., thanks).

If this sounds horrifyingly familiar, you should be embracing the online dating scene instead of hating on it. If you're strapped for time and know you're attached to your Blackberry/iPhone anyway, what's the harm in sending a few messages here and there? You won't have to waste your time going on countless dates to find out if you share the same basics values and goals as the other person; you can cut to the chase and weed out the wrong ones right from the beginning.

Online dating is also a great way to meet people you wouldn't have met otherwise. Why limit yourself to meeting through friends, or through your parents, or leaving finding your soulmate up to fate? That only happens in a Katherine Heigl movie, anyway. If you're daunted by the sheer size of sites like Match.com and eHarmony, don't be daunted.

The online dating industry rakes in upwards of $2.1 billion a year.[3] It's such a moneymaker that competitive new niche sites are popping up every single day. At this point in time, there is, quite literally, something out there for everyone.

But how do you know which site is right for you? Your options are only a click away!

3   *PR Web.* February 7 2012. <http://www.prweb.com/releases/2012/2/prweb9159292.htm>

CHAPTER 2:

WHICH SITE IS RIGHT FOR YOU?

Do you remember the days when there were so few available sites that online dating seemed like a rare and very weird beast? You probably even remember the days when it was acceptable to troll for respective partners on Craigslist (which I think is totally unacceptable these days.) Thankfully, the days of being relegated to Yahoo! Singles and its prehistoric brethren are finally over, and you can freely pick and choose depending upon what's important to you.

Are you religious? Do you only like Australian women? Is it a requirement that you only date other single parents? Maybe you have "unusual" sexual tastes and get off on guys that wear Tigger costumes. My point is, there's something out there for everyone.

I know, I know, with so many choices, how is possible to even fully know what's out there, much less which site is right for you? It's exhausting try-ing to track down that perfect fit – and we aren't even talking about partners here yet. Luckily, I'm here to help. So without preamble, let's get this party started. RIGHT?

THE BIG DADDIES

1) **Match.com (http://www.match.com)**

   The Breakdown: Match.com is the most rec-ognized dating site on the Internet. It doesn't discriminate against anyone; all age groups and sexual orientations can make matches here. The sign-up process is virtually pain-less, though you will be asked to create one of those annoying "About Me" essays. Once you fill out your member profile, you'll be present-ed with daily matches of people who should (in theory) be perfect for you. If you don't like/aren't attracted to your matches, you'll still be able to search for other, **less compat-ible** people.

   Number of users: More than 30 million users in over 37 different countries worldwide.

   Who You'll Meet: The average Match.com user is a middle-aged white woman with chil-dren with an average income. That said, you can – and will – meet anyone on this site. The male/female ratio is split pretty cleanly down the middle with ever-so-slightly more women at 51/49.

Matches made: As of 2009, Match reported that 12 couples on average get married or engaged every day.

Cost: A one-month membership costs $39.99, but prices decrease depending on how many consecutive months you purchase at once.

Pros: Match is reasonably priced, has a huge database of users and deposits daily matches into your inbox each day. If you sign up for a six-month membership plan right off the bat and don't find anyone you like within that time frame, the site gives you an additional six months of use for free. It's also easy to navigate, has fun features and allows you to IM with other users.

Cons: You have to pay for a plan to really take advantage of the site: if you don't subscribe, you'll only be able to wink at your matches, which gets you absolutely nowhere.

2) eHarmony (http://www.eharmony.com/)

The Breakdown: eHarmony is the site best known for making marriage matches. That said, the sign up process is so lengthy that you probably want to be serious about settling down or committing to someone if you're going to join this site. You'll have to fill out an extensive questionnaire when you start -- that's 436 questions measuring 29 areas of compatibility – and will have to answer additional questions before you and a match can even begin emailing. Same sex couples can't find a mate here, though the company did launch the gay-friendly site CompatiblePartners.com in 2009. It's possible that straight folks might not find a match on eHarmony, either, though: it is possible that you can be deemed "unmatchable." At that point, there's nothing more the site can do for you.

Number of Users: Over 20 million worldwide.

Who You'll Meet: eHarmony has a high number of female users: 66 out of 100 percent.[4] Forty-six percent of all users earn over $60,000 and are over the age of 35. These are financially secure individuals who are serious about settling down.

4   *eharmony Stats 2009*, 2009, <http://www.datingsitesreviews. com/article.php?story=eHarmony-Releases-Stats-Update-2009>

Matches Made: It has been reported that, as of 2009, 236 American members were, on average, getting married every day.[5]

Cost: At $59.95 per month, eHarmony is a bit pricey – but, like most other dating sites, the more long-term a plan you buy, the cheaper the cost becomes.

Pros: It takes so much time to initiate contact with someone that those who aren't completely serious about meeting someone are weeded out; you won't have to worry that you're going to meet someone who just wants to play around. The eHarmony team also guides you through every step of the dating process, including arranging a secure phone call in case you're leery of giving out your digits and forcing you to send introductory "get to you know" messages before you even communicate by direct message. You can narrow down exactly what you're looking for by defining your "must haves" and "can't stands" (deal breakers) as well.

Cons: If eHarmony can't match your with another user, you're completely out of luck. There's really no other reason to use the site, as you won't be allowed to search for matches on your own.

5   *Harris Interactive/eHarmony study.* February 7 2012. <http://www.eharmony.com/press/release/82005>

3) Plenty of Fish (http://www.pof.com/)

The Breakdown: Plenty of Fish is the most globally visited dating site, which has as much to do with its relatively low cost as it does with its ease of use. In comparison to Match.com and eHarmony, Plenty of Fish has more of a real community, grassroots feel, though by contrast is also has fewer bells and whistles.

Number of Users: 40 million users worldwide.

Who You'll Meet: The site's users skew a bit older with an average age of 39, though it is widely used by those in their twenties and thirties; it is used by more women than men.

Matches Made: No concrete numbers have been published, though millions of couples have left Plenty of Fish with at least one relationship under their belt since the site's 2003 launch.

Cost: Most of the site's basic functions are free, though you do have the ability to become a premium member for a relatively low cost. You also have the option of purchasing Goldfish credits, which allow you to buy add-ons. One such feature is the Read Message, which allows you to see if your message has been read or not. With Goldfish credits, you will also have the ability to send virtual gifts

Pros: Most of the site's basic functions are free. Rival sites will make you pay to view profiles, send messages and chat via instant messenger. There's also a huge and very active database; you have options.

Cons: There are always dangers to using a site that's almost completely free (beyond your date being a cheapskate, that is). If you do choose to become a premium member, a one-month option isn't available: you'll need to sign on for at least three months up front (though, at $7.60 a month, it won't exactly break your bank).

BEST OF THE REST

1) **Spark (http://www.spark.com/)**

The Breakdown: Come on baby light your fire? Maybe…if you're lucky. Spark plays the dating game by allowing members to look for love any which way they want it. The site, which professes to be a "fun site for serious daters," keeps itself fresh by using a color-coding system. You'll take a quick personality test to establish which color you are, which, ostensibly, helps you build "a deeper and stronger" relationship with the people you choose to meet.

Number of Users: Over one million.

Who You'll Meet: There's something for everyone here. The site is non-exclusive and caters to all age demographics

Matches Made: Undetermined.

Cost: It's free – such a good flavor!

Pros: Many people will be happy with the free price tag and the fact that they'll be able to respond to emails without having to purchase an expensive membership to do so. Spark also requires that all members post pictures, which cuts down on posers and cheaters (you'll see why later).

Cons: Leaving users up to their own devices sounds like a good idea, but serious daters might be turned off if there's absolutely no indication as to why they should connect with another. Sparks can fly when you're superficially attracted to someone, but where can a relationship go when that singular bond of attraction is gone? That's right: it goes "bye-bye!"

2) LavaLife (http://www.lavalife.com/)

The Breakdown: Not everyone is at the same place relationship-wise or looking for the same thing. Therein lies the strength behind LavaLife: there's something for everyone. It's easy to narrow down exactly what you're looking for given that the site caters to those looking for a relationship, casual dating or an intimate encounter.

Number of Users: In the thousands.

Who You'll Meet: Anyone you want. This site is a great tool for meeting people locally, as it's basically an online personals ad. Single parents have said that they have the most success looking for love on this site as well.

Matches Made: LavaLife doesn't make the matches for you and doesn't require you take a personality test to find who you might be a fit with. Finding the right person to date is left entirely up to you.

Cost: It's free!

Pros: LavaLife is easy to use and, as I've mentioned before, has something for everyone. It's easier to weed out those men looking simply for an "intimate encounter" right from the get-go if you're seeking a serious relationship.

The "Quick Facts" listed right up front make it easy to eliminate people straight away, as well. For example, if you don't like smokers and you see that Ted1901 is physically you're type but chain smokes like a chimney, then you can automatically cross him off your wish list. The site also has an Instant Messenger capability and the option of integrating your Twitter feed with your profile is offered as well.

Cons: Several users have complained that LavaLife is for those who would rather hook up than have a serious relationship.

3) Friend Finder (http://friendfinder.com/)

The Breakdown: Friend Finder is distracting in a good way. There are so many things to do, so many options available and so many connections to be made that you'll wonder if it's more of a social networking site or a dating site. But don't be fooled: though there is an element of networking going on, it's definitely for those seeking "friends" of a sexual and romantic nature.

Number of Users: More than 450 million people use location-specific sites globally. There are 1.1 million paying, active members in America.

Who You'll Meet: Maybe you'll get lucky and have a relationship, but finding a friend with benefits is almost guaranteed.

Matches Made: Undetermined.

Cost: There's a basic free membership included, but you won't be able to communicate with members. Therefore, you'll have to buy a silver or gold membership which will run you at least $20 a month.

Pros: The site updates itself every 24 hours, so the number of users is actually accurate. It's also a great way to meet people in your area and fun to use, as well, with interactive features like daily horoscopes, photo ratings and e-greeting cards. Although non-paying members can't initiate contact, paying members can, for an additional fee, purchase an add-on that allows the cheapskates to communicate with them alone for free. It's a win-win situation for all involved (especially the penny pinchers).

Cons: Though the number of users online are announced on the site's homepage, "online" is an ambiguous term. It can mean that the user in question was online anywhere from an hour to 24 hours before. Additionally, Friend Finder users have complained about a surplus of fake profiles.

4) Date.com (http://www.date.com/)

The Breakdown: Date.com is a lot like Friend Finder. It's an online personals site that caters to people looking for love locally. You can get to know someone in an online chat room, or even create your own private online conversation den in order to get to know someone a bit more intimately. You may not find love here, but if you're looking for a simple hook-up or a little attention from the opposite sex, this is as good a spot as any.

Number of Users: There are reportedly 7 million users on the site with 35-55 thousand more joining, on average, each week.

Who You'll Meet: Just about anyone. There are many options here, so you can say you're looking for love, casual dating or an "intimate encounter."

Matches Made: Undetermined.

Cost: A basic membership is free, but you'll need to upgrade to a gold membership in order to send any messages.

Pros: There's a large pool of members to choose from, and it's generally assumed that most members are upfront about what they're looking for.

Cons: Most features aren't available unless you pay for a membership, though, even if you do have a paid membership, you're limited to 50 messages a day.

5) Perfect Match (http://www.perfectmatch.com/)

The Breakdown: Perfect Match is *not* for the casual dater. The site's Duet Compatibility System is designed for a more mature adult that's actively seeking a relationship. After an online interviewing process, the user will be set up with a few select matches based on a series of scientific algorithms which are meant, ostensibly, to find you that "perfect match" you've been so desperately seeking. The site is also unique in the sense that it offers video dating profiles called "Dating on Demand," which allows others to see you in action.

Number of Users: Five million users with rapidly increasing numbers thanks to publicity given from appearing on programs like *Live With Regis & Kelly* and the *Dr. Phil Show*.

Who You'll Meet: Although people of all age demographics use the site, its fastest growing age group is the 50+ set. Happily, the male to female ratio is currently 50/50.

Matches Made: Undetermined.

Cost: At $59.95 per month, Perfect Match is a bit pricey but, like other dating sites, the longer you choose to subscribe, the cheaper the monthly rate becomes.

Pros: Although you're only matched with a few select people, you still have the ability to seek others out on your own. Members also have the opportunity to ask the site's co-founder and relationship expert, Dr. Pepper Schwartz, direct questions.

Cons: Personality profiles will take you a good 15 minutes to fill out, so make sure you've put aside enough time to join. Also, several users have complained that they're constantly being matched up with users who have no profile pictures and/or are out of their location ranges.

6) **Zoosk (https://www.zoosk.com/)**

The Breakdown: Though Zoosk started off as a Facebook application in 2007, by 2010 it was listed by comScore.com as the number one most used dating site in America (though it no longer holds that title). It's for those social media friendly, which means that its members

– whom refer to themselves as Zooskers – can communicate with one another via iPhone, MySpace, Facebook and Twitter.

Number of Users: Over 50 million in over 60 countries worldwide.

Who You'll Meet: It's popular with thirty and forty-year-olds, but given how social media-friendly it is, college-age daters are also fans.

Matches Made: Undetermined.

Cost: Like most sites, the longer you subscribe, the cheaper Zoosk becomes. One month costs $29.95 but a three-month package evens out at $19.95 per month. Additionally, you can purchase Zoosk coins, which, at 10 cents each, unlock additional features on the site.

Pros: All members can reply to emails sent by premium (paying) members. Also, Zoosk can pull information off of any of your current social networking sites, making profile creation simple and painless. Photos are required to flirt with other members, so it's rare that a photo-less (and thus potentially sketchy) user will contact you. The coin system is also quite cool, as you'll be able to do things like send virtual gifts, special delivery flirts, communicate with a user via email and bump up your profile – called a Boost View – so you'll be moved to the top of the search list and thus receive more messages.

Cons: There isn't a matchmaking system available, so you'll have to find your perfect match all on your own.

7) **OKCupid (http://www.okcupid.com/)**

The Breakdown: The beauty of OKCupid is that it tells you just how compatible you are with another user, but allows you to contact those you're blatantly not right for anyway. You'll be told exactly how you link up with every single user and the percentage of which you're a match, friend or enemy. Should you fall for the looks of an "enemy" and get your heart broken, you've made your own mistake. You can also rate others based on a star system: if you and another rate each other highly – four or five out of five stars – you'll both be sent messages saying that you're attracted to one another and should probably get in touch. The hard work here is done for you, as you have, essentially, an entire website acting as your own personal Cupid.

Number of Users: Over a million users in America alone.

Who You'll Meet: The majority of OKCupid users are 18-34 year-old white males with a college education and an income of $30K or less. Young professionals, college students and more mature individuals use the site, as well.

Matches Made: An undetermined number, though users do post their success stories on the site.

Cost: It's free, though additional features are available for the fee of $9.95 a month.

Pros: It's free to use without restrictions. You can still contact, respond to and "like" other members without paying. There's also a "toy box" full of personality quizzes and other interactive online games you can play. You can tell when someone's been checking you out, as well.

Cons: A free site has its upsides and downsides, one being that the users – like most online sites – are not screened first. Also the flipside to knowing when someone is looking at your profile is that they can also see when you've been checking *them* out.

8) Chemistry (http://www.chemistry.com/)

The Breakdown: The creators of Match.com are the brainchildren behind Chemistry, a sister site that's based on the science of compatibility to make your matches. In addition to answering traditional questions about yourself and the person you want to date, you'll be asked to look at pictures and complete puzzles in order to ascertain who's the best fit for you. Based on your responses, you'll be placed into one of four categories with a correlating sub-category, and thus able to decide who you *should* be dating and who you definitely need to avoid.

Number of Users: A whopping 15 million.

Who You'll Meet: Sure, more than half of the users are women between the ages of 35-49, but that still means they have a 60/40 shot at making a chemical reaction[6].

Matches Made: A handful of marriages and engagements have come from matches made on the site so far.

Cost: It's super expensive to sign up for Chemistry: a one-month subscription costs $49.95, which only becomes $26.65 per month if you sign up for a six-month plan.

6 Quantcast.com , January 2012, <http://www.quantcast.com/chemistry.com>

31

Pros: The personality test alone is worth signing up for the site, as you'll discover hidden insights about yourself and about the person you're most compatible with – though perhaps *you* aren't even fully aware of what it is you want yet. You'll also be alerted whenever another member is interested in you. You also have the option of going inactive whenever you want, be it because you've met someone you like on the site or because you simply need a break from online dating.

Cons: Annoyingly, you will want to check out your matches, but you cannot do so unless you're a paid member. Its cost is also another downside; Chemistry's one-month trial subscription is the highest I've seen.

CHAPTER 3:

MATCH.COM vs. EHARMONY

When newbies to the online dating community are deciding on a site, they typically go with what they know (or at least what they've heard of). The two most recognizable names in the online dating game are easily Match.com and eHarmony. Both sites have huge numbers, big marketing campaigns and competitive prices. That said, even simply selecting which of the two is right for you is a hard choice to make.

Although they might seem alike in theory, in reality Match and eHarmony are as different as apples and oranges (or pears and grapes, vodka and milk, vanilla and chocolate and so on). Typically, those that join each are looking for a differentiating level of commitment, which makes the process of picking one over the other a whole lot easier than you'd assume.

So here comes the big breakdown: serious daters should head to eHarmony, while those that are looking for a relationship or to casually date should opt for Match.

When I say that eHarmony is for the "serious" dater, I mean that quite *seriously*. It's for those that are ready to settle down and be married, like, yesterday. Their theme song should be Beyonce's "Put a Ring on It." This is not to say that Match.com isn't a marriage-friendly site: it is. However, those that sign up for Match aren't only looking to tie the knot and start popping out babies. They do so because it doesn't require a huge commitment and allows them to a) try online dating for the first time rather painlessly and b) see what options are out there. These people are single and ready to mingle, but not necessarily ready to stop sowing their wild oats. This could change on a dime, however, if the right person comes along.

Each site takes a different approach to the getting-to-know-one-another process. eHarmony requires its users to link up slowly, so that they might make more of a connection through shared interests over time. After filing out a lengthy questionnaire, users aren't allowed to immediately start chatting; they have to answer a series of questions about themselves first. If they *still* want to meet, only then will they be allowed to start emailing.

Match.com's dating pool is much larger and its questionnaire much less demanding. There's not only more of a variety to choose from, but you can easily go after people you're attracted to as opposed to those you're compatible with but find completely unappealing. The experience is much less time consuming and (dare I say it) more fun for the new online dater, given that it's almost like shopping for a date/mate. Given that attraction is a big part of any relationship – found online or otherwise – it's rather confining that you're unable to browse through users on eHarmony.

On that note, it should be said that those who are choosing between the two might also opt for Match because it's cheaper. Those who aren't as intent on finding a serious partner might be put off by eHarmony's high price tag, which, at $39.95 is double Match's monthly rate.

Again, it really all depends on what you're looking for, how serious you are about finding love and what it is, specifically, that you want out of your experience.

This nifty little chart should better help you make your decision.

$\longrightarrow$

	Match.com
Cost	* 19.99
Age of users	25.3% are under 30; 50.4% are 30-49; 24.3% are 50+
Education of users	75% have some college or college degree
Matching technology	A simple matching system allowing you to browse other members who might not be a fit
Communication with other users	Open communication: contact who you want, when you want, how you want.
Target dater	Generally those who are looking for dating/relationships
Number of users	More than 30 million
Smartphone friendliness	Match.com Mobile allows members to search, flirt and connect with other eligible singles through their mobile phones. Offerings are available through AT&T Wireless, Nextel and Sprint, and free apps are offered on all major Smartphone platforms including iPhone and iPad, Blackberry and Android.
Extra features	Match has a plethora of fun extra features. With Match.com Platinum™, a personalized, professional matchmaker is available for users who don't have the time to weed through user profiles. Also, with MindFindBind™, you'll get advice from Dr. Phil, who will tell you how to mentally prepare for a date, how to find someone perfect, and then how to strengthen your relationship with Mr. or Mrs. Right. Match also offers the free online magazine *Happen* for tips on dating as well as love advice.
Taking the test	You'll fill out a pretty basic profile section which includes: interests, lifestyle and values as well as an About Me essay section. A personality test is offered, but is not a requirement of signing up for the site. Features like Singled Out and the Daily 5 are available so serious users can better discover their best fit.
Searching	Again, you'll have 100% free reign to pick and choose.
Navigation	Simple and painless.

* Based on purchasing a three-month plan

eHarmony.com
* $39.95
38% are 18-34; 41% are 35-49; 21% are 50+
47% had a bachelor's degree[7]
An advanced matching system based on a 258-question test; compatibility based
Controlled communication: eHarmony walks its users through a step-by-step process that introduces singletons over time.
Generally those who are looking to get married.
More than 20 million
eHarmony does have both an Android and an iPhone app available. eHarmony HD is also available to make the online dating experience easier for those who choose to access the site through their Smartphones.
eHarmony has an entire site devoted to doling out advice and dating called eHarmony advice. You'll find helpful articles discussing common dating mistakes and how to fix them, as well as get tips on how you should act on a date and how to tell if a person is interested in you. You can also take quizzes that will tell you what you're doing wrong, what type of person you should look for and what type of person you should avoid.
The eHarmony profile is one of the most extensive found on any online dating site. With 436 questions measuring 29 dimensions of compatibility, the profile will take you about 40 minutes to complete. Think of it as a multiple-choice test with a couple of short open responses thrown in. There isn't an essay component involved.
You can't – eHarmony manages your matches. If there isn't anyone that matches up with you, sorry, but you're out of luck.
Simple and painless.

7   Allen, Marshall, March 6 2004, <http://www.eharmony.com/singles/servlet/press/articles?id=26>

THE EHARMONY/MATCH USER FACEOFF

Now that you know what both eHarmony and Match have to offer, I thought you might want to read some reviews of some people who have tried both. After surveying 100 people in the age ranges of 23-35, I have to conclude that Match was the overwhelming favorite.

But again, do what's right for you based on what it is that you're looking for. Or, better yet, try both!

LAURIE, BOSTON

"I've ultimately decided that online dating really isn't for me at this point in my life, but I have to say that I really, really, really hate eHarmony. I did not meet one attractive person on that site. The point of online dating – for most people – is to meet someone that you want to be in a relationship with, who you're also attracted to. But there was no chance at all that that was going to happen for me on eHarmony.

"It's like hearing that 75% of the population is completely undateable. I know where those undateable people went: eHarmony. Though I will say that that attractiveness is not universal. The uniqueness of relationships, of meeting people, is that there is somebody for everybody. We don't always find our friends' significant others to be attractive. In addition to being unattractive, most of the men that contacted me were really weird as well. Trust me, I have no problem with being a geek – I like smart men – but these guys went above and beyond the point of 'strange.'

"I also hated that eHarmony only shows characteristics when someone comes up as a match, not a phone; apparently the site doesn't want us to judge people by how they look. You have to click on someone's page to see his entire profile. The rub *there* is that these guys can tell when you've looked at his page, and, when you do, they usually contact you.

"Let me give you an example. I was matched with this 36-year-old guy, which is fine because he was in my desired age range. He was 5'9, which was *not* my desired height, as I'm tall. He had half a head of hair; the other half was MIA. In one of his pictures he was hugging a tree. I think that description pretty sums up for me why I dislike the site – that's not someone I would ever date, and I was pretty specific about it. I'm riding out my subscription – I bought three months up front – but now I'll only go online when I need to feel better about myself."

• •

MEGAN, MIAMI

"I never actually went on any dates when I subscribed to eHarmony – I didn't really find any of the people attractive. I don't hate it though, it was amusing. But I will say that I genuinely loved Match.

"I'm really tall, so it was a blessing to me that I could get rid of people based on their height. I didn't want to date someone that was shorter than 6'1 and I was really specific about it. You can essentially tailor make your man and get a lot of responses and results back.

"Plus, on Match, it seemed like when you talked to people, they would actually talk back. People actually communicated more than just a one-line email saying, "Hi, let's meet up even though we've said exactly the equivalent of two sentences to each other.'"

• •

BETTE, LOS ANGELES

"I prefer Match because you clearly have more options and you have the ability to browse people's profiles, while eHarmony is pretty restrictive. They send you matches for you and you alone.

"When I went on a date with a guy from eHarmony, I was like, "What did I put in that computer that made them think I'd be compatible with this idiot?" I think he must have BS'd his way through the whole test.

"I think women are more apt to be honest and put everything out there on those sites, while men tend to lie. I will say that one of the guys I met on Match lied by an inch. When I asked him why he lied and said that one inch didn't make a difference at all, he told me that women get alarmed when they see 5'9. Weird.

"I prefer Match because you can look and see if you're physically attracted to the person, and then look and see if his profile fits the bill, too, though I also do think that the people on Match are looking to hook up more than the people on eHarmony are. Though I'm in a relationship now, if I had to do it all over again I'd choose Match over eHarmony for sure."

● ●

HAYLIE, BOSTON

"I definitely preferred Match, mostly because creating your online profile was much easier. You write what you're looking for in a man and your interests, where you've traveled to and your dislikes. An important thing for me was easily being able to sift through the available men before shelling out money for a monthly or yearly account. For me, Match was totally worth every penny; there were always a lot of new faces and great matches – I did have a lot in common with the men I was matched with.

"I also liked that there were so many people using the site. I figure the bigger the pool, the better a chance you'll have to meet someone. I think it's great that Match offers suggestions of people you should date, though you can easily say 'No, thanks' if the guy isn't your type physically. Or, if you found a hottie you weren't matched with and wanted to talk to, you could 'wink' at him as opposed to putting yourself completely out there by sending an email. It's a good way of showing someone that you're checking him out and still letting him do the work by putting the ball in his court."

• •

ANDREW, LOS ANGELES

"If I had to choose eHarmony or Match, I'd go with Match.

"eHarmony wasn't free form enough. It doesn't allow you the opportunity to choose and look. It gives you what it wants to give, which might be different from what you might want. Just because you have X criteria with someone doesn't mean you're going to get along. My dates were just whatever. There was no magic on either end and they didn't really go anywhere. The whole process was too long and drawn out. You send me something, I send you something. It was like in sixth grade when you sent notes back and forth and then checked off boxes with, 'Do you like me? Yes or no.' It was annoying.

"Match is slightly better because it's more user-friendly, although it does seem like it's for people who mostly just want to get laid. I don't know whether I want a relationship, sex or a commitment from any of these girls. I still haven't figured that out yet. I do know that I'm mega picky, and the kind of woman I like ultimately isn't on Match. However, I can say that it's been an interesting experience in terms of finding out what I do and don't like. I've discovered that I like my women to be a little more bohemian, a little quirkier, a little more contemporary. The girls I've met on Match are far too square-peggy for my tastes."

• •

LACEY, LOS ANGELES

"Although I didn't mind Match, I like eHarmony much better. I felt like whenever I met someone on Match, it was like, 'Let's hook up' or 'Do you want to have sex tonight? Because I do.' They want to meet after you've been talking to them for about five minutes, which barely gives you time to know anyone at all. The guys I went on dates with wanted to move too fast for me.

The people on eHarmony are definitely looking for relationships. I preferred it because *I* was looking for a relationship. It weeds out the people that aren't serious about looking for love with the long questionnaire you have to fill out and the endless back and forth questions, plus it's also more expensive than Match."

* *

HARRY, LOS ANGELES

"I've had an eHarmony account for the past few years, and I definitely prefer it to other sites I've used like Match and OKCupid. What's nice about eHarmony specifically is that you're only given seven profiles a day, which isn't an overwhelming amount to look at. On Match, you can search through hundreds of people and it becomes really time consuming. You'll spend hours going through profiles and do it all over again a week later, forgetting that you've actually seen someone's profile before realizing not only that you wasted your time, but that a girl you're not even interested in can tell that you've looked at her profile twice like a stalker.

"It's just so easy on eHarmony. The first stage of communication is five multiple-choice questions. The site saves the answers you like, so it only takes two clicks of your mouse and you've sent a girl you think is attractive a message. You don't have to spend a half hour thinking about what to say in a well thought out email. It's more efficient time-wise if you're busy.

"I will say that I have had the intention of stopping online dating altogether and cancelling my eHarmony account, but then I always forget and another six-month membership rolls over. But if I am going to be online dating, I prefer eHarmony to a free site like OKCupid, where you definitely get what you're paying for."

●●●●●●●●●●●●●●●●●●●●●●●●

I CHOOSE NEITHER!
WHY JENNIFER IS QUITTING
ONLINE DATING AFTER
SEVEN YEARS, SIX SITES AND 50 DATES

"I have been using online dating sites since 2004 and trust me, I've tried them all. You name it, I've done it: Match, eHarmony, Plenty of Fish, Chemistry, OKCupid and even FaceMatch.com. But it's time for me to go into online dating detox. I haven't met anybody good yet and I finally know that I'm not going to – online, at least.

"I admit it, I'm big into looks; all my friends say I'm picky. I like nice teeth and nice skin. I like a guy who's educated, who has a job, a good income and who went to school.

"But after using all of those sites in all these years, I've been out with two people who were even just OK. That's two dates out of fifty.

"On Chemistry, there were two guys out of 2,000 profile pictures that I found attractive. I went out with one of the two – an orthodontist. The date was going well; he was actually as good-looking as his picture indicated, and so I broke my first on-line date 'no kissing' rule. I regretted it immediately afterward when he said, 'Do you stand naked in your window?' That was the first and last time we ever went out.

"As for eHarmony, well, I called them and complained that I wasn't getting any quality matches, and they offered me an extra six months free to stay. I told them 'no thanks.' I'm done.

"I feel like I'm outgoing and smart and have a lot to offer someone. The people I was meeting online didn't have anything to offer me. Some were uneducated, some lied about their pictures and some weren't at all who they said they were, whereas I'm completely honest. I don't try to be something I'm not; you either like me or you don't.

"I'm so done right now. I'm 35. I want to meet

someone, but there's so much pressure with on-line dating, and it can be so discouraging. I don't want to have to think about it, I just want to meet someone and have it be easy. I signed up for these sites because I thought it was easier than meeting someone out in the real world, but I was wrong."

• •

CHAPTER 4:

THE BEST NEW DATING SITES

It's a universal rule that no two people are the same, so why should everyone be using the same few dating sites? The three sites below are innovative, creative and less stressful to use for those who live in fear of filling out the online profile. So without further ado, let me present my favorite new(ish) niche sites.

1) **How About We (http://www.howaboutwe.com/)**

The Breakdown: This dating site cleverly lets you pick a partner based on the things you enjoy doing. You can either fill in the blanks yourself by suggesting a date (re: How about we…go for a bike ride around Central Park and then grab a burger at Shake Shack afterwards) or browse the users who have already posted, looking for someone with common interests.

Who You'll Meet: People that like doing things, being active and having fun as opposed to the serious dater who's looking for love as their be-all-end-all goal. Ninety-eight percent of its users are educated, with a Bachelor's Degree or higher, and fall between the ages of 29 and 35.

Cost: Memberships costs anywhere from $8 to $28 per month.

Why It Works: This is a great site for a city dweller who likes to be up on the latest hot spots, see the latest films and check out hip new art exhibits. In addition, you can always think up new ideas for dates. You also have the ability to search for matches based on gender, age and location. It blends the concept of online and off-line dating in a natural way. How About We also offers a companion blog, The Date Report, which features similarly edgy, mainstream talk about modern day dating.

2) Nerve (http://dating.nerve.com/)

The Breakdown: Nerve is a site for those who might be looking for the person of their dreams, but aren't so dedicated to the cause. The sign-up process is easy and amusing. Instead of answering basic questions regarding your future, the site keeps things fresh and fun. For example, a standard dating site would ask how you feel about kids, giving you the options of "I want them some day" and "I have kids." On Nerve, even answering this sort of standard question will make you giggle out loud. "I have kids somewhere," "I have kids, but they're at home" and "I'm not interested in kids" are a few of your choices.

Who You'll Meet: Cute and funny hipster types, as well as those who are interested in talking about life as opposed to endlessly talking about themselves.

Cost: $20 per month, though a free 14-day trial period is offered.

Why It Works: Some people still feel that a stigma exists when it comes to online dating, and Nerve is a good place to alleviate any lingering online prejudices. Ostensibly, it's a site where people can communicate and have interesting chats about virtually any topic out there. As the site's mission statement reads: "Nerve Dating isn't going to feed you an algorithm, because in our opinion, algorithms don't lead to love. We just want to help you talk about interesting things with interesting people. The rest is up to you." Also, for those that absolutely hate talking about themselves (as opposed to talking about things, places and pop culture), you won't have to write that dreaded "About Me" section.

3) Cheek'd (http:// http://cheekd.com/)

The Breakdown: Cheek'd is a game changer; a site that professes to be "online dating, reversed." Signing up goes like this: You purchase a deck of cards from the site, on which are written clever, sarcastic phrases like, "Act natural. We can get awkward later" or "Don't over think this." The idea behind the deck is to slip an attractive stranger the card, which will have your name and an online code on the back. If the receiver is intrigued, he or she can log their code online and send you a personal email.

Who You'll Meet: Anyone you damn please. Literally.

Cost: A deck costs $20; there is also a monthly subscription fee of $9.95, which you can cancel at any time.

Why It Works: It's completely safe, as the card receiver never has your personal details, and it's a great way of breaking the ice. Plus, it allows you to feel bold, brazen and confident by making contact with that person you mightn't have had the courage to speak to otherwise.

AN INTERVIEW WITH CHEEK'D FOUNDER LORI CHEEK

"I was out to dinner with a friend one night, and I saw this really hot guy give a girl his card. His number was written on the back. I remember loving how mysterious a gesture it was, and immediately after I had a light bulb moment. I thought, 'How many times have I made eye contact with a guy somewhere and wish I had said something?' This was how the idea behind Cheek'd was born and eventually grew into what it is today.

"It isn't a typical dating site; it's a game changer. Match.com's slogan is 'One in five people find love online.' Well, our new slogan is going to be, 'What about the other four?' There are billions of single people out there, and not everyone is doing the same online dating thing.

"Online dating is so serious. It's like having a full-time job. People that are doing it seriously spend nine hours a day behind their computer. When they're off of work, what do they do when they want a date? They go straight back behind their computer. With these cards, you actually get yourself out there; you'll be doing things and living life. You can be cheeky, have fun and see if you have chemistry with someone. There's a sense of humor behind Cheek'd, which is rare, considering that there aren't that many dating sites that aim to make you laugh. Laughing really is the best icebreaker.

"You can have atypical experiences with these cards. I can take them on a plane to Shanghai and they'll still lead whoever I give them to wherever in the world back to me. I do, of course, use them myself. In fact, I see half the people that receive my cards again.

"Don't be mistaken, though it's a great tool if you're shy, it isn't *just* for shy people. There are so many opportunities out there where you just can't say hello to someone you like. If you're riding the subway in the morning and a guy has his headphones on, you're not going to walk up to him, ask him to take off his headphones, tell him he's cute and ask him to go out with you. You're not going to walk up to a man who's having a business dinner with four associates and interfere in his conversation. These cards are also a way of avoiding missed connections and a way of creating mystery and intrigue.

"For example, I was having dinner at a restaurant in Manhattan, and I recognized a famous French documentary filmmaker sitting at the table next to me. He was clearly on a date, and it didn't look like it was going well. I noticed that he had a winter coat on the back of his chair, and that his pocket was gaping wide open. So I slipped a card saying, 'Our fate is in your hands' into his jacket pocket. When he found the card five days later, he messaged me using the code on the back and wrote that he was 'intrigued.' He asked me to meet him at the Whitney. It didn't work out in the long run, but the point is that I physically took fate into my own hands, as can you. Why try the standard approach to online dating? You can never substitute the chemistry you have in person for what you might find from behind a computer."

CHAPTER 5:

NICHE SITES

Sometimes the big daddy sites are just so overwhelming that you have difficulty making a choice. It's like going into a Starbucks for the first time, hemming and hawing over what you want for fifteen minutes before giving up in frustration and grabbing a black coffee with sugar at the deli next door.

That's where niche dating sites come in. If something is so important to you that it eclipses everything else, why try a general site? Surround yourself with like-minded individuals.

There are sites that cater to every possible thing and every possible person you can think of. Are you an animal enthusiast? Try out Catloversdating.com or PURRsonals.com. Is it important to you that you and you love match share the same faith? Log on to Christiansingles.com or Jdate.com.

I know that even knowing where and what to look for can be overwhelming, which is why I've made a big old list of niche sites for each and every type of user possible. Don't freak out – breathe deeply and slowly. While you're meditating, think about what it really is that you want and what it is that's important to you. Once you've got that down, the online dating world is your oyster.

A MASTER LIST OF NICHE DATING SITES

International Men of Mystery

1) Asian Dating
   (http://www.asiandating.com/)

2) Aussie Cupid
   (http://www.aussiecupid.com.au/)

3) Badoo (http://badoo.com/)
   "Meet new people!" (in your area)

4) Canadian Personals
   (http://www.canadianpersonals.net/)

5) Date British Guys
   (http://www.datebritishguys.com/news.php)

6) International Cupid
   (http://www.internationalcupid.com/)
   "Find your international beauty"

7) Japan Cupid (http://www.japancupid.com/)
   "Serious Japanese dating and relationships!"

8) Lonely Soul (http://www.lonelysoul.net/)
   "A perfect date with your soulmate"

Holier Than Thou

1) Catholic Match
   (http://www.catholicmatch.com/)
   "Grow in faith, fall in love"

2) Christian Café (http://christiancafe.com/)
   "Proudly Christian owned"

3) Christian Mingle
   (http://www.christianmingle.com/)
   "Delight yourself in the Lord and
   he will give you the desires of your heart"

4) JDate (http://www.jdate.com/)
   "Meet Jewish singles"

5) LDS Singles (http://www.ldssingles.com/)
   "Seek and ye shall find..." (Mormons, that is)

6) Love and Seek Christian Singles
   (http://www.loveandseek.com/)

7) Muslima (http://www.muslima.com/)
   "Muslims for marriage!"

Oh, Behave! A Touch Of Kink

1) Alt.com (http://alt.com/)
   "The tighter, the better"

2) Daily Diapers
   (http://www.dailydiapers.com/)
   "Age play, fetish wear & diaper lover
   community"

3) Diaper Mates (http://diapermates.com/)
"Diaper lover personals"

4) Furry Mate (http://furrymate.com/)
"Where real relationships begin"

5) Vampersonals
(http://www.vampersonals.com/)
"The #1 dating site for vampire
& gothic single personals"

Where Co-Eds Can Get Their Online 'Education'

1) College Passions
(http://www.collegepassions.com/)

2) Student Love
(http://www.studentlove.com/)

3) Date My School (http://datemyschool.com/)

4) Campus Hook
(http://www.campushook.com/)

5) Fall Terms
(http://www.fallterms.com/)

6) University Love Connection
(http://www.universityloveconnection.com/)

In The Navy (Or Army, Whatever)

1) Military Cupid
   (http://www.militarycupid.com/)

2) Military Friends
   (http://www.militaryfriends.com/)

3) Military Singles
   (http://www.militarysingles.com/)
   "The dating site for single soldiers…
   and those interested in meeting them"

Age Is Only A Number

1) Age Match (http://www.agematch.com/)
   "Age is just a number"

2) Cougar Life (http://cougarlife.com/)
   "The ultimate catch"

3) Senior Match
   (http://www.seniormatch.com/)
   "Find love again"

4) Senior People Meet
   (http://www.seniorpeoplemeet.com/)

5) Silver Singles
   (http://www.silversingles.com/)

6) Yes! Mrs. Robinson
   (http://www.yesmrsrobinson.com/)

Love At Any Size

1) Large Friends
   (http://www.largefriends.com/)
2) BB People Meet
   (http://www.bbpeoplemeet.com/)
3) BBW Personals Plus
   (http://www.bbwpersonalsplus.com/)
4) Cuddly Lovers
   (http://www.cuddlyloversdating.com/)

Amorous Pet Owners

1) Cat Lovers Dating
   (http://catloversdating.com/)
2) Date My Pet
   (http://www.datemypet.com/)
   "Date me. Date my pet."
3) PURRsonals (http://www.purrsonals.com/)
   "Where cat lovers greet and meet"
4) Equestrian Cupid
   (http://www.equestriancupid.com/)
   "Keep away from the city –
   enjoy rural and country life"

Race Specific

1) Amor (http://www.amor.com/)
   -- Latin dating
2) Black People Meet
   (http://www.blackpeoplemeet.com/)
3) Indian Friend Finder
   (http://indianfriendfinder.com/)
4) Interracial Match
   (http://www.interracialmatch.com/)
   "Love me, love my color"

Same Sex Singles

1) Compatible Partners
   (http://www.compatiblepartners.net/)
2) Gay Cupid
   (http://www.gaycupid.com/)
3) Gay Dating (http://www.gaydating.com/)
4) Pink Cupid (http://www.pinkcupid.com/)

Scoring Richie Rich

1) Established Men
   (http://establishedmen.com/)
   "Where the beautiful and successful meet"
2) Millionaire Match
   (http://www.millionairematch.com/)

3) Seeking Arrangement
(http://www.seekingarrangement.com/)

4) Sugar Daddie (http://sugardaddie.com/)
"Where the classy, attractive
and affluent meet"

5) Sugar Daddy For Me
(http://www.sugardaddyforme.com/)

Looking For One Thing Only
(Hint: It Isn't Love)

1) Passion (http://passion.com/)
"Sexy personals for passionate singles"

2) Online Booty Call
(http://www.onlinebootycall.com/signup/)

3) AshleyMadison.com
(http://www.ashleymadison.com/)
"Life is short. Have an affair"

4) Horny Wife (http://hornywife.com/)
"Horny wives looking for affairs"

When No One Else Will Date You
(Because You Have An STD)

1) Positive Singles
(http://www.positivesingles.com/)
"Stay positive! Find love, support and hope"

2) 1 in 4-date (http://1in4-date.com/)
   "Got herpes? Who cares? So do we!"

3) Prescription4Love
   (http://prescription4love.com/)

4) Poz Personals (http://pozpersonals.com/)
   "What you need to know to
   find that someone special"

Kids Come First

1) Parent Fishing
   (http://www.parentfishing.com/)

2) Single Parent Love
   (http://www.singleparentlove.com/)

3) Single Parents Mingle
   (http://www.singleparentsmingle.com/)

4) Single Parent Meet
   (http://www.singleparentmeet.com/)

Geek Lovin'

1) Brainiac Dating
   (http://www.brainiacdating.com/)
   "Where it's sexy to be smart!"

2) Cupidtino.com (http://cupidtino.com/)
   "Meet an Apple fanboy or girl"

3) TrekPassions.com (http://trekpassions.com/)
   "Love long and prosper"

4) GK2GK (http://www.gk2gk.com/)
   "Find your geek match"

5) DateCraft (http://datecraft.com/)
   -- For World of WarCraft fans

6) Nerd Passions (http://nerdpassions.com/)

The Beautiful People, The Beautiful People

1) BeautifulPeople.com
   (http://www.beautifulpeople.com/en-US)

2) Darwin Dating
   (http://www.darwindating.com/)
   "Online dating minus ugly people"

Vie For A Veggie

1) Green Friends
   (http://www.greenfriends.com/)
   "Where vegetarian friends and
   singles feel at home!"

2) VeggieDate.org (http://veggiedate.org/)

3) VeggieRomance.com
   (http://www.veggieromance.com/)
   "Find your other half"

4) SingleVegetarians.com
   (http://www.singlevegetarians.com/)
   "A vegetarian is a person who won't eat
   anything that can have children"

Political Passion Play

1) Democratic Singles
   (http://democraticsingles.net/)
2) Conservative Dates
   (http://www.conservativedates.com/)
   "Where conservatives meet"
3) Liberal Hearts
   (http://www.liberalhearts.com/)
4) Republican Passions
   (http://republicanpassions.com/)

Jail 'Birds'

1) Women Behind Bars
   (http://womenbehindbars.com/)
2) Inmate.com (http://www.inmate.com/)
3) Meet an Inmate
   (http://www.meet-an-inmate.com/)
   "Lonely inmates in the USA seek penpals"

Size Matters

1) Height Site (http://heightsite.com/)
   "For tall people and the
   people who love them"

2) Little People Meet
   (http://www.littlepeoplemeet.com/)

3) Midget Dating Service
   (http://www.midgetdatingservice.com/)

4) Short Passions
   (http://www.shortpassions.com/)

5) Tall Friends (http://www.tallfriends.com/)

Weird, Yes. But They Do Exist

1) StachePassions.com
   (http://stachepassions.com/)
   "Oh yeah, it's all about the 'stache!"

2) FarmersOnly.com
   (http://www.farmersonly.com/)
   "Meet thousands of down to
   earth country folk today!"

3) BikerKiss.com (http://www.bikerkiss.com/)
   "Two wheels, two hearts, one road"

4) Gothic Match
   (http://www.gothicmatch.com/)

5) Indie Dating (http://www.indiedating.net/)

6) Uniform Dating
   (http://usa.uniformdating.com/)
   "Online dating for anyone who works in uniform or likes those who do!"

7) Shy Passions
   (http://www.shypassions.com/)

8) Tattooed Singles
   (http://www.tattooedsingles.com/)
   "Where body & art connect"

9) Wine Lovers
   (http://www.wineloversmatch.com/)
   "Meet wine loving singles and discover the wine life"

10) Date Ginger (http://www.dateginger.com/)
    "Actually, redheads have more fun"

11) Redhead Passions
    (http://redheadpassions.com/)

12) ALikewise (http://alikewise.com/)
    "Dating based on book tastes"

13) The Atlasphere
    (http://www.theatlasphere.com/)
    "Connecting lovers of
    The Fountainhead and *Atlas Shrugged*"

14) You and Me Are Pure
    (https://www.wewaited.com/)
    "The friendly place for virgins to meet"

15) Rez Me Now (http://rezmenow.com/)
   "Second life residents community"

16) 420 Dating (http://420dating.com/)
   "Why toke alone?"

17) Poly Matchmaker
   (http://polymatchmaker.com/)
   "The perfect place to find your poly mate(s)!"

18) Sea Captain Date
   (http://www.seacaptaindate.com/)
   "Find your first mate!"

19) Tastebuds (http://tastebuds.fm/)
   "Tell us the music you love to find
   people nearby who share your tastes"

20) Find Your Face Mate
   (http://www.findyourfacemate.com/)
   "21st Century Matchmaker: Research shows
   that people are more likely to be attracted
   to others whose facial features are similar to
   their own"

LAUREN'S STORY:
I'M CATHOLIC, BUT I SIGNED UP
FOR JDATE TO MEET JEWISH MEN

"I was raised Catholic and went to Catholic school my entire life, but I've always been into Jewish guys. I'm obsessed. There's just something about them. I like their looks – their dark features, curly hair, tan skin and dark eyes – but most of all, I seem to find that most of them have this great, sarcastic, fiery sense of humor. Being able to make me really laugh is such a turn on. So I guess you could say that I have a type.

"I've been using online dating sites for a few years now. eHarmony, Match, Plenty of Fish, OKCupid…I tried them all. But I wasn't really meeting the kind of guys I wanted to be. All the men I met on those sites were only semi-attractive, so I decided to give JDate a look.

"I mean, wow. The guys on JDate are so hot, that I decided to just bite the bullet and sign up though I didn't really like the fact that I had to pay for it. But I guess any amount of money is worth it to meet the kind of man I've always dreamed of marrying.

"The loophole here, because I'm not Jewish (yet) is that I checked a little box saying that I'd convert. It's a great way of getting around that pesky religion issue. It's true that I went to Catholic school, but I'm sure any potential love interest isn't going to be that hard on me, as I'm not religious now – and willing to change for him! Plus, I took three Judaism classes in college and kept all my books. The man of my dreams is bound to be impressed by *that*, wouldn't you say?"

CHAPTER 6:

COMPUTER, COMPUTER, ON THE WALL, MY FAVORITE DATING SITE OF ALL IS...

Drum roll, please! Yes, a little suspense *is* necessary here. Of all the dozens of sites I've sifted through and tested out, there is one that I believe is a cut above the rest. So without preamble, I'll give out my favorite dating site award to...Chemistry.com!

Dr. Helen Fisher, who does triple duty as Chemistry's chief scientific adviser, a professor at Rutgers University and a biological anthropologist, actually created the site's incredibly fun and unique personality test. Her theory is that every human is primarily comprised of two out of four different personality types. We are all a combination of the following: an Explorer, Negotiator, Director and Builder.

Understanding your type helps you understand who you fall in love with, why people act the way they do in relationships and why or why not someone might be right for you. By under-standing yourself, you can choose what kind of person is going to give you what you need.

First, let's talk about the types.

♥ **The Explorer** (ruled by dopamine) is adventurous, novelty-seeking and creative.

♥ **The Builder** (serotonin) is cautious, conventional and managerial.

♥ **The Negotiator** (estrogen) is empathetic, idealist and a big-picture thinker.

♥ **The Director** (testosterone) is aggressive, single-minded and analytical.

Fisher, who has been studying love for over 30 years, has concluded that the following attractions exist: Explorers like other Explorers and Builders opt for other Builders, while Negotiators and Directors do the opposites attract thing.

Explorers go for like-minded individuals be-cause they crave excitement that only someone who's as thrill-seeking and creative as they are can understand. They're optimistic and curious, love adventure and want a partner who craves a similar spontaneity. The only drawback is that Explorers tend to avoid deep discussions like the plague, as they're not entirely comfortable talking about their feelings.

If you find your Builder match, you're lucky: they're not only the most likely to marry each other, but also the most likely to say they're happy, as well as the least likely to divorce. They enjoy bringing people together and are successful at building large circles of friends and keeping their families happy and secure.

Last but not least, Director/Negotiator matches are drawn to one another because they're such complete opposites – yins to yangs, if you will. Negotiators see the big picture while Directors are far more detail-oriented. They're also compatible socially, as Negotiators have the ability to smooth over (and don't mind doing so) the more aggressive comments made by Directors.

Discovering which type you are is also a fun – albeit lengthy – process: it *will* take you anywhere from 20 minutes to a half hour to complete the test, so set aside some time for your personal discovery.

While taking the test, you'll have to answer questions like "When I see two people kissing in public, I'd rather not look" and asked to gauge how strongly you feel. Other questions that help establish your true personality type include: "What color best describes my personality?" and "I vividly imagine horrible things happening to me."

Later, when you've actually subscribed to the site and want to get to know more about your matches, you can open with quirky conversation starters that actually *would* break the dating ice, online and off. You can open a fortune cookie by answering how it would apply to your life and then asking your match to the same or cutting to the chase and taking a "Relationship Essentials" test which quickly helps you discover if you're on the same page and looking for the same things.

Of course, Chemistry isn't perfect by a long shot. Like every dating site, there will be dissatisfied users. The dating pool here is much smaller, and paying members will become just as frustrated as those who join for free. You may see someone you like on the site, but they won't be able to contact you back unless they pay up, which, at a monthly rate of *$49.95[8] is pretty pricey (and what I consider to be the big fly in its ointment).

What's great about Chemistry is, that though you know who you should be dating because of your personality profile, that doesn't prevent your from contacting other members and vice versa. It's up to you, using the information you've been given, to make an informed decision as to who you should date.

That said, I've discovered that most Chemistry users have no clue what the personality test is actually *for*. They think, "It's another cool dating site, and it was created by the same

••••••••••••••••••••••••••
8   * Based on paying for a one-month membership only

73

people who did Match, so, sweet. I'll try it." Sorry people, but you're missing the point completely if you don't understand what type you are or who you should be dating. Why go for a Builder/Director if you're an Explorer/Director? Sure, he might be cute, but you already know your personalities aren't going to mesh. If the point of looking for love online is that you're really seeking to meet someone special, then shouldn't you at least try and see if the science behind the site works?

On that note, I strongly advise you to buy Fisher's book *Why Him? Why Her? How to Find and Keep Lasting Love* as a companion piece to understanding the science behind Chemistry.

I'm going to excuse myself now because I just geeked out for an entire chapter, because I'm a big believer in Dr. Fisher's scientific theory. Understanding yourself, as well as others, is a key component in finding the right relationship. And really, aren't you ready to create a chemical reaction?

AN INTERVIEW WITH CHEMISTRY.COM CHIEF SCIENTIFIC ADVISOR DR. HELEN FISHER

"The brain is the ultimate matchmaker; it has its own algorithms. What I do on Chemistry.com is take a look at the patterns of personality in the brain to find out why you gravitate towards certain people over others.

"There are four chemical systems linked to personality traits; dopamine, serotonin, estrogen and testosterone. If you're expressive of the dopamine system, meaning that you're novelty seeking, curious, spontaneous and liberal, I call you an Explorer. Builders are expressive of the serotonin system. They're conventional, popular, orderly, meticulous, religious and respect authority. Directors – represented by testosterone -- are analytical, direct, decisive and very good at engineering, mechanics or music. Negotiators – estrogen – see the big picture, are imaginative, intuitive, compassionate and trusting.

"Of these four systems, I've found that explorers are attracted to other explorers, builders other builders, and negotiators and directors have that opposites attract reaction. A good example of a director-negotiator match would be Hilary and Bill Clinton. She's the director here – high testosterone, forthright, gets the job done. When she was asked why she was initially attracted to Bill, she said, "Because he wasn't afraid of me." Bill is the negotiator here. He's the one who can't stop talking, feels everybody's pain and cried at their daughter's wedding. It's a case of opposites attracting.

"Brad Pitt and Angelina Jolie are perfect examples of two explorers matching. They whiz around on motorcycles, lead unconventional life-styles, have lots of children without being married. This is also why he didn't work out with Jennifer Aniston; she's much more the stable, traditional, conventional builder type.

"Understanding who you are and who you're drawn to is a crucial factor behind the science of Chemistry.com. If you can understand who you are in terms of these types, then you can not only understand important things about yourself, but you can anticipate what the future will look like with whoever you're dating and who would be a good partner for you.

"We're all flailing about when it comes to on-line dating profiles. We're looking at the way the people in the pictures look, they way they smile. I'm trying to make people realize that taste and at-traction go deeper than a simple photo and give them a window into the brain so they can under-stand who and what will work for them.

"There are no bad combinations, per se...but by understanding the different personality types, you'll understand what you're in for. Sometimes you really don't want someone like yourself. We don't know what happened in one another's child-hoods. You may crave the safety and reliability of a builder if you're an explorer who was raised by an explorer parent. What we're trying to do is give you the ability to make an informed choice.

If you're an explorer who goes for a builder, you need to expect that when you want to have a last minute nude fling in the park, that your partner is going to want to sit there and watch television instead. It doesn't mean he isn't attracted to you; that's just who he is, so anticipate it.

"What separates Chemistry from other dating sites is that it's based in science. Most dating sites understand the basic patterns of nature. Their algorithms match you on similar values, education and looks. But you have to understand that there are two parts to personality, and that the basics alone won't necessarily create chemistry. There's your environment – what you grew up to do, say and think – and then there's your biology – your inherited traits. Most dating sites measure your cultural interests, but I'm trying to bring the second half of the puzzle into the game. I want you to understand, through this second half, that you're not going to be able to change the other person. You can't make a curious person uncurious or a restless person domestic or a cautious person adventurous. It's part of your DNA.

"I want you to remember two important things: first, there's only one real problem with dating on the Internet, and it's called cognitive overload. You begin to believe that there are thousands of people out there for you, and the more people you check out, the less likely you are to end up with any of them; you literally get overloaded with data. You believe, because you have so many options, that there is the perfect person for you out there, and you begin to nitpick. If someone seems great but has curly hair over straight, which you prefer, you don't pursue. So my advice is this: after you meet nine people, pick one person and get to know them so you don't get into a morass of constantly looking for the new and getting so overloaded that you don't find anyone at all.

"Secondly, think of reasons to say 'yes.' We're always thinking of reasons to say no! When you first meet someone, you overweigh the few things that you do know. For example, you crack a joke and when the other person doesn't laugh, you instantly think they have no sense of humor and you couldn't possibly marry someone who's so humorless. You jumped way ahead and overweighed. So unless it's totally obvious that you aren't going to work out, overlook the small things and think of reasons to say yes instead.

"There will always be magic to love, to meeting that person you have amazing chemistry with. However, by helping you to understand how the brain works, we're giving you a better chance of making love last."

PART II:

TIPS & TRICKS FOR CREATING THE PERFECT PROFILE

CHAPTER 7:

HOW TO CREATE
THE PERFECT PROFILE

If you're serious about looking for love, know that you need to devote some serious time, thought and energy into your online profile. If you're not willing to dedicate a measly hour or two into looking for love the modern way, then you probably aren't ready to be part of a committed relationship in the first place. So continue on your merry way trying to pick up/trying to get picked up at a bar. I hope you feel good about yourself when you can't find your underwear or self-respect in the morning.

Say what?! I'm just trying to weed out the losers who have obstinately made up their closed-minded little minds that they will never, ever try online dating. Weeding out the losers is part of what, you, too, are going to have to do in the very near future, so listen up if you want results (or if you really and truly don't know whether saying you like long, romantic walks on the beach is a good idea or not).

If you learn nothing here, please at least remember this one, crucial thing: you're advertising *yourself* in your profile, so keep it real, and keep it honest. Nobody wants to be a victim of false advertising.

What's In A User Name?

If I never have to see a HotStud696969 or BigPete8675309 again in my life, I will be the happiest woman alive. Choosing a user name isn't the most important part of creating your online dating profile, but it can be one of the most off-putting if you don't get it right.

I'm not just calling out the guys here, either. For some reason, many women find the need to include "sexy" or "sweet" or "blue-eyed" as adjectives before their series of random numbers. Is it wrong to do this, per se? No. Is it as annoying as hell? Um, yes.

There are, of course, tricks and tips to picking an eye-catching, attention-grabbing, non-vomit-inducing username.

Don't choose anything that may be construed as egotistical. HottestGirlintheWorld87 may have a few problems when her dates beg to differ that her user name is highly debatable and, in fact, she's made one hell of an idle boast.

Do make a list of interesting adjectives that really define you. You have to convey *something* about yourself, after all. Some good, fun words are: sharp, quick, nimble, sprightly, swift, audacious, fearless, gutsy, defiant and euphoric.

Don't go numbers crazy. The user name you want may be taken, but that doesn't mean you have to whip out the digits as if they're going out of style. Three will suffice, but two is ideal.

Do make a list of nouns to complement your adjectives. Instead of adding your name, street or town to your username, why not list your favorite instrument, fairytale character or color? Using your profession as your noun of choice is acceptable though totally snooze-inducing. Yeah, you're immediately letting people know what you do, which will score you points if you're a doctor or a lawyer, but you won't be considered much of a catch by revealing that you're MaleExoticDancer93. Funny/quirky names are much more successful.

Top Taglines

Again, the tagline isn't the most important part of your profile, but its placement at the top of your page means it won't go unnoticed. Given that it will be one of the first things a potential suitor sees, make sure it's a good one!

Funny quotes from your favorite book, song or movie are always crowd pleasers. Girls, if you reference anything from *Anchorman, Elf* or *Old School* (any Will Ferrell film will do, actually) a man may not be able to help himself from checking out your profile. For practice, randomly approach a male friend with nothing more than "I love lamp" or "60% of the time, it works every time" and see how he reacts.

If you don't feel like quoting a guy-friendly film, write something innocuous like, "I love cheeseburgers" or "Conquering Brooklyn one pizza joint at a time." No, you won't sound crazy – just fun.

Conversely, you can also use the three adjectives that best define you. Keep it short, sweet and simple (though FYI, those particular three words *aren't* the best choices for your profile). The point of your headline is to provoke discussion, create some form of ice breaker or to reveal who you really are, so keep that in mind when you're creating.

Above all else, ladies, please remember this: do NOT put anything akin to "Looking for Love," "The best girlfriend you'll ever have," "Seeking Prince Charming on White Horse" or "In search of Mr. Right – is he you?" in your headline. *No* man in his right mind would want the job with a headline like that. Guys, I feel like I shouldn't have to say this (but I probably do, because you're men):

never, ever announce in your headline that you want a hot and sexy fling. It's an online dating site, for cripes sake! If you want a porno partner, there are other better places to find her.

About Me

What sets you apart from the pack? On paper (or online) everyone has the ability to sound vaguely similar, but in life no two people are exactly alike. It is our unique experiences that shape us and make us individuals. How's that for a tall order? How does one sum up their very existence, the very core of who they are, in 500 measly little words? The About Me section is probably the most irritating part of creating an online profile, unless you happen to be a narcissist who loves to talk about him/herself for endless amounts of time.

When writing your profile, make sure to let your voice really be heard so that your personality is literally leaping off the page. I know, I know, that sounds hard and this section sucks, but you really don't want to completely ignore it. Find ways of making it less like a college essay and more ways of making it fun.

Instead of droning on about yourself, tell a story. Instead of saying something mundane like "I work in PR," reveal how you dreamed of being an astronaut/ballerina/mad scientist, and then add in a self-deprecating way, "I was a dreamer, but I found myself working in publicity. Hey, I started off simple. And, if I'm being honest, I really think my motivation for my first choice of work was the helmet/tutu/goggles." Be original. It goes a long way in the world wide web of unoriginality.

On that note, you need to have a really classic opening line/paragraph. By classic I mean "killer." You need to hook the object of your online affection with your dazzling wit or pure chutzpah.

Open with something that says who you are in a positive and genuine way. Instead of saying "I'm a 31-year-old woman who loves the nothing more than to curl up on the couch at home watching re-runs of *Beavis & Butthead*," say "I've been to Morocco, Australia and Cambodia, but still think there's no place quite like home...especially when *Beavis & Butthead* are on TV and my take-out sushi place finally gets my order right (it hasn't happened yet but I'm holding out hope)." You aren't being negative or boring and have effectively showed that you have a multi-faceted personality. You're interesting...and he should want to know more.

Here is the most important piece of advice I can offer regarding the "about me" section: Never, ever write that you have a "good personality." Even if you do, you'll still sound like the kind of person who was picked last in gym class. This is especially important for a woman to remember. A guy will think back to all those times one of his female friends tried to set him up, and when he asked "So, is she hot?" his gal pal would exclaim "She's got a great personality!" He will remember (incorrectly, of course) that the girl he was forced into meeting blindly had horns, a tail and caterpillar eyebrows (though she really only had a cleft palette). He will run past go without even collecting his $200. "Go" being you, in this case.

Likes/Dislikes

If something is a huge part of your life, don't hide it: include it. Part of partnership is accepting the other person for who they are. That isn't to say that you immediately need to reveal all of your flaws or weird quirks, but if something is important to you, don't hold back.

Some examples: you might be an avid churchgoer who wouldn't dream of missing a Sunday service, or a person who faithfully follows Phish around the country. These things are what you love and aren't willing to give up, so you'll want to make mention of these things in your profile through your written profile or photographs. Either way, if someone can't accept that you're a guy who goes on yoga retreats twice a year or that you're a girl who competitively mud wrestles, that person isn't the right one for you.

Gals, although it is impressive that some of you can so freely express yourself, don't go overboard and make a man think you're on the verge of spinsterhood. Saying that you like every single Drew Barrymore or Reese Witherspoon movie ever made is the dating profile equivalent of chopping off a guy's manhood and feeding it to your cat. In case you don't get what that means, here's the Cliff Notes version: he ain't gonna be into it.

Use the dislike section as an opportunity to be funny and/or tongue-in-cheek. You don't ever want to be the girl that says she dislikes cheaters or liars or megalomaniacs or even guys that leave the toilet seat up. Guys, never say you can't stand a girl who shops. We all shop, even if it's just for groceries. You're going to sound like a jackass. Instead, say that you abhor something ridiculous, like Astroturf or Tickle Me Elmo. It gives the other person an in to talk about your utter ridiculousness (or for you to realize how moronic the other person really is if they seriously ask, "So wait, do you really hate Astroturf?")

The Perfect Partner

This section screws up a lot of would-be relationships from the get-go, so I'd refrain from putting too much effort or work into it. Girls, you don't want to be so specific that you look picky and high-maintenance or so overly romantic that it looks like you're living in a Taylor Swift-style fantasy world. Again, if a deal breaker is involved (re: you're Jewish and need to marry a Jewish man), then by all means, include that. You want to weed out the bad and be specific about the good. There's no need to say that you specifically want a man with Ryan Gosling's abs; there's no way any man can compete with that and they won't bother trying to.

Gentlemen, be genuine. Women are going to see right through your crap if you profess to be a "sensitive guy just looking for love." Can somebody please pass the barf bag?

Sports Savvy

If you're one of the increasingly large number of women who care about boys who play with balls, use it to your advantage. What do men love more than sex? Exactly. Watching boys playing with balls while drinking a Bud. This tactic is working for the women of New Zealand, so it should work for women elsewhere in the world, as well. Forty-three percent of all gals using the Kiwi website FindSomeone [9] scored when they

••••••••••••••••••••••••

9   *McDonald, Greer.* October 21, 2011. <http://www.stuff.co.nz/life-style/blogs/who-gives-a-ruck/5823304/Rugby-to-cure-man-drought>

used the word "rugby" in their profiles. The only caveat here is this: if you aren't into football, baseball or their brethrens, don't pretend to be. Your lack of knowledge *will* be rumbled immediately, and though guys won't think you're a bad person for lying about knowing one linebacker from the next, they will think you're a liar. If you *are* one of the Gridiron Girls[10] – the increasingly large number of women who consider themselves to be diehard NFL fans – power to you, good for you – now use it in your online profile. When you've added that in to the "About Me" section, take your beer and cheers yourself to successfully scoring on all accounts.

Give Honest Answers To Basic Questions

The problem most women have with online dating is that many don't think of what it is that *they* want, but what is going to make them seem the most desirable to the opposite sex.

Be honest about what you want. Most sites have clear-cut yes or no answer options to questions like "Do you want kids" or "Would you date a smoker?" There are deal breakers and then there are things you can actually deal with. Decide what's important to you and answer as such. If

....
10 *Baker, Katie.* January 30, 2011. http://www.nytimes.com/2011/01/30/magazine/30FOB-wwln-t.html

you refuse to answer such things as "Do you drink on a regular basis?" you're essentially answering "Yes" anyway, so why refrain from telling the truth?

A Change Will Do You Good

When you first join a dating site and you've got an interesting profile, the powers-that-be decide to highlight how cool you are. You should enjoy that time in the spotlight, because it won't last for long. The longer you're on any given site, the more of a regular you become. If the same old profile keeps popping up, you're going to keep on getting ignored in a "been there, looked at it, didn't like what I saw so kept moving" kind of way.

It's always good to assess how many responses you're getting and how many people seem interested. If you're getting a lack of online love, don't fret. It isn't you – it's your profile and the amount of time you spend online.

Those who are more active have an elevated position in other users' search results. The people who've forgotten they even joined a dating site in the first place aren't going to get a reminder in the form of much inbox love: the less you're online, the less you'll be contacted by others.

You might want to change your situation by changing up your "About Me" section, as well. Try new things. Switch your profile picture, spruce up your headline, try being a little funnier. See what works for you, and what the opposite sex responds to.

OKCupid, in particular, has an awesome application called My Best Face, which lets other users rate which of your pictures they prefer the most. Why not put your best foot (and face) forward?

Politics

There's a steadfast rule that when you're in a bar and you're drunk, you avoid talking about three things: sports, religion and politics. Although, as we've already discussed, it's prudent to mention the former two categories in your online dating profile, research has found that the Barack Obama doesn't make for a warm bedfellow (unless you're Michelle Obama, that is).

One study[11] reveals that singletons attempting to find a boyfriend or girlfriend online usually leave their political leanings off of their profiles. In fact, only 14% of the 2,994 people polled felt confident enough to disclose their political stances.

More than half of that number refrained from actually owning up to a love of donkeys, elephants

....
11 *Melina, Remy.* September 20, 2011. <*http://www.livescience. com/16134-daters-avoid-revealing-political-preferences.html*>

or any other such beast, describing themselves as "middle of the road." Those who were most pragmatic about their political choices were older users, who described themselves as "very liberal" or "ultra conservative."

Nary a one admitted to any personal feelings for Sarah Palin. Just saying.

Please Remember, One Last Time...

Regardless of how cool and fun you are, you aren't going to click with everyone. Don't get disheartened if you don't always get a reply, or if communication stalls after a few half-hearted messages. It isn't *you* – it's him or, more specifically, you and him together. If it's right, it's right and if it's not, don't fight it.

CHAPTER 8:

DATING PROFILE PHOTOS DO MATTER

Let me ask you a serious question: how many times have you turned down a setup because the person in question was described as "nice" as opposed to hot, stunning, or good-looking? When you pressed, you got the response "Looks aren't everything," which pretty much validated your rejection. Don't be ashamed to admit that you've been there and done that, because we've *all* been superficial in our lives at some point.

So how does this apply to online profile pictures? Well, in most situations, you won't even get the chance to prove how "nice" you are, because you're being judged on one thing and one thing only: your looks.

Even if you've put loads of thought, time and effort into your "About Me" section and have proven yourself to be unique, cool and hilarious, if your photos are duds, it's all over before it's even begun. You'll be dismissed with one quick click of the mouse, and the potential partner of your dreams will move on to more physically appealing pastures.

Before you get all "that's so shallow," you should probably also admit to yourself that you've done – and consistently *do* – the same thing. Appearances are important. You wouldn't date someone that you aren't attracted to, would you? For those who need me to actually spell it out, the answer here is: no, you cannot. The other person might not be the most aesthetically pleasing person on the planet, but he or she *must* be attractive to you.

Therefore, you're going to want to put your best – and most honest – face forward. Meaning: most of you aren't going to upload a photograph where you're posing in an elegant gown twirling a strand of pearls and sipping daintily from a glass of champagne. That isn't *you*, it was a Halloween costume or your cousin's wedding. Don't misrepresent. If you wake up dripping in diamonds and Aqua-net, power to you, Audrey Hepburn.

For those of you who are less *Breakfast at Tiffany's* and more McMuffin shoved-in-mouth-on-way-to-work (that is, to say, *normal*) here is all you need to know about picking the right kind of photos for your profile.

1) **Smile! Actually, don't.**

A recent study[12] found that men actually prefer women who make flirtatious faces or show off big, toothy smiles in their profile pictures. What they *dislike* is for you be looking oh-so serious and/or to avoid making eye contact with the camera. Can you blame them? By refusing to grin, you look like a buzz kill... or a female serial killer. And although you may think you look arty or wistful by looking away from the lens, you actually just come across as a woman who's ashamed to show her face. So play coy, tilt your head just a little, think something naughty and smile directly into the camera. Don't say cheesy as you snap.

2) **Full Frontal**

At the end of the day, guys are easy. They want to see gals looking sexy – not to be confused with slutty -- and they want to see *all* of you. Before you go getting all indignant, reread my first statement. They don't want to see you naked (right away, that is), but they do want to see your entire body. They want to make sure "the goods" exist, so to speak. Opt for a full-length or three quarter length

••••••••••••••••••••••••••
12   *Rudder, Christian.* January 20th, 2010. <http://blog.okcupid.com/index.php/the-4-big-myths-of-profile-pictures/>.

picture. In case you're thinking that it's so un-cool for a guy to judge you on your body, riddle me this: how cool is it of you to conceal the fact that you're actually twenty pounds heavier than you've claimed to be? He's going to be so disappointed backslash disgusted that he's never going to call you again anyway. It will save you a lot of hassle in the long run if you refuse to lie about who you are or what you look like. If he's not interested in the real you from the get-go, he's not going to be – and why should you settle for less?

3) **The 'MySpace Photo'**
Oddly enough, men *really* dig the so-called "MySpace Photo." I'm talking about the shot all girls love to take, shot from above on an angle. Yes, cleavage can usually be seen. But it isn't just a bit of booby that gets guys all hot and bothered. This horrific shot is alluring because it looks a little bit dirty. Stay with me here and don't get grossed out, but it reminds them of what you're going to look like while you're doing the deed. Plus, if it was taken on a cell phone camera, guys are typically going to assume that it's recent. Weird, yes, but it does work.

4) Get In His Bed
(Or Your Own, Whatever Works)

Shocker of the year: men like the thought of you in bed. Yeah, I know, I'm astounded too! Being photographed in your rumpled sheets is a major turn on for men. They envision you doing the nasty together and, in turn, get themselves all hot and bothered. You suddenly become a whole lot sexier in their eyes... even if you're actually wearing flannel footie pajamas beneath the sheets.

5) The Great Outdoors

Just like guys dig the thought of getting you into bed, they also appreciate the thought of you exerting yourself by doing something active and sweat-inducing. Although hiking, mountain-climbing or surfing isn't exactly all that and a bag of sex, men associate active movement with bumping uglies. Don't ask me why – that's just the way the weird male brain works. But make sure the majority of your photos aren't taken in the evening: men are going to think you're hiding something by refusing to show yourself in broad daylight.

6) Lovely Jubblies

I've got another newsflash for you, so you might want to stop the presses: men like boobs. If your mammary is turning up in any kind of online photo, a guy (and his guy) are going to stand up and take notice. In fact, one[13] study shows that cleavage-baring shots earn women 12.9 new contacts a month, which is 49% more than average. And no, age doesn't matter. Boobs are still boobs, regardless of how high or low they go.

7) Lions, Tigers and Bears – Oh My, That's Why You're Still Single!

I love cats, despite the fact that a pussy is the universal sign for "sad, single and alone." However, I will never, ever again pose with a feline friend for that very same reason. Men don't see your affection for animals as adorable: they think of you as that sad, single cat lady you've always secretly feared you'd become. Even if you have kitty friends at home, don't pose with them. You can tell your nine tabbies how well the date went after it's actually happened.

8) Gorgeous Girl Groups Suck

If you've ever been to a bar with a gaggle of girlfriends and wonder why, at the end of the night, no one has approached you, here's the

13 *Rudder, Christian.* January 20 2010. <http://blog.okcupid.com/index.php/the-4-big-myths-of-profile-pictures/>

reason: you're unintentionally intimidating. Penetrating a plethora of girlfriends to get to a girl they find attractive is the equivalent of breaking into Fort Knox for most men. But that isn't why he's going to avoid messaging you, oh no. Men typically go for the brightest, shiniest toy in the room, so if he sees you surrounded by six of your prettiest pals, he's likely to go for whichever one of the girls in the picture sparkles the most. If that isn't you, he might find you dull by comparison. He might think to himself: "Wow, that hot blonde is way cuter than *this* girl. Does *she* have an online profile?" I'm not telling you to a) pose with unattractive friends or b) go out and find unattractive friends if you don't currently have any – I'm just saying keep the real beauties out of your online profile pictures. Nobody should put Baby in comparison corner, after all, especially if the comparison isn't going to work in her favor.

9) Show And Tell Totes Stopped Being Cool In Elementary School

You admit it: you're cool. You've done a lot of truly excellent things in your life and believe that any potential partner should be impressed by the greatness that is you. However, in the wild world of online dating, he probably won't be. Showing that you've bungee jumped in New Zealand or hung out with Colin Farrell might be impressive, but it also leads a guy to believe that you have an elevated opinion of yourself (which may not be completely warranted) or that you actually *are* too cool for him. In which case, you don't really care what he thinks, do you?

10) Boozebags Are Bad

If you're over 21 (OK, who am I kidding? Humans start drinking pretty much as soon as they've exited the womb these days) you enjoy a tipple or two on occasion. But although a guy likes to see breasts, he doesn't want to visualize the other part of the *Girls Gone Wild* experience, the drunkenness. Although many of the not-so-nice guys will use online dating as an easy way to get you into bed, if a man harbors the illusion that you could be the mother of his child or the good girl he's going to one day bring home to his own mom, your affinity for the hard stuff will be a turn-off. He'll think you're just another silly party girl. If he's attracted to you, you still may receive a message and/or get asked out on a date, but beware of his motivation. He might be contacting you with the express intent of getting you into bed and never to be heard from again ever after, amen. Why put yourself in a situation that could have been easily avoided? Like G.I. Joe says, "Now you know, and knowing is half the battle."

11) Have One (A Picture, That Is)

Trust me, if your profile has no picture, men are going to gloss over you as if you don't exist. You might have the wittiest, most clever profile in the world, but no one will read it unless you give him something aesthetically pleasing…or at least *something* visual to focus on. As a rule of thumb, you should have at least four recent photos on your profile to prove that you are who you say who you are and that the photographs are all recent.

Were you beginning to think that I'd leave the boys out? Hardly! But you gents might have to start stripping down while I'm talking…

1) Take (Most) Of It Off

Though you might initially think that ladies are too smart and serious to be into something as blatant and sexually provocative as a shirtless photo, I'm not proud to admit that we appreciate a nice chest the same way that you do. But for the love of God gentlemen, please only show off your muscles if you have them!

This is not a mandatory photograph and it doesn't work for everyone.

2) Keep It Real...Simple

Trying too hard to impress us by wearing suits, tuxedos, cummerbunds or Mr. T-style gold chains (that was a joke) typically has the opposite effect. If you've got to put on a shirt, make sure it's simple, like a T-shirt or a button-down with jeans. A fancy outfit is going to lead us to believe you're high-maintenance. For the record, your gender doesn't have a monopoly on disliking that particular personality trait.

3) Do Be A Lover (Of Animals)

Although similar shots don't work when the sexes are reversed, ladies love to see a man's sensitive side. Whether he's posing with a cat, dog, dolphin or parakeet, women can't help but to say 'aw' when she sees a guy posing with his pet.

4) The Universal Lie: Why A Guy Should Never Pose With Hot Girls

Listen up guys, and listen well. If one of your male buddies tells you that you'll attract more attention by appearing with a bevy of scantily clad beauties, you've been sadly misinformed.

Women aren't thinking, "Well that girl is attractive and he hangs out with *her*, therefore I, too, should be impressed by his good looks." No! She's going to wonder how many of those girls you've hooked up with and how many other women she's going to have to compete with for your affection. We like a challenge *within reason* – but if we know the odds aren't stacked in our favor from the very beginning, we're not going to play the game. Capisce?

5) The Not-So-Great Outdoors

I know you think you look rugged and manly while you're hiking Runyon Canyon, but guess what – Bear Grylls you're not. Women prefer to see you doing something interesting, like reading a book, wine-making or even painting than see you posing next to a tree (being associated with a tree-hugger only works if you're a hippie). Similarly, we'd much rather see you in your true natural habitat – hanging out with your buddies – than see a snap of you posing next to your good friend Big Ben.

CHAPTER 9:

TIPS & TRICKS FROM THE EXPERTS

Creating the perfect look for your online dating profile picture is serious business, which is why I've enlisted the crème de la crème of fashion, beauty and makeup professionals to help out. Go big or stay home, right? Check out these tips and tricks to maximizing your profile picture potential from the likes of *What Not to Wear* host Stacy London and world-renowned makeup artist Sue Devitt.

MARILYN COLE, CELEBRITY STYLIST & ALTERNA SPOKESPERSON

ADVICE FOR WOMEN

"In the long run, men are looking for 'natural' women, or what they think is natural, but is, in fact, enhanced. Men love volume and length, but they don't want that length to be faked. If they know it's an extension, they'll think you're high-maintenance, which is a turn-off. However, most men are naïve, and if the results are good, they won't have a clue that your hair isn't real.

"In order to achieve that full, long, natural look, use a volumizer. One of my favorites is Alterna's Bamboo Volumizing Mousse. Rough-dry the product into your hair and then, once it's dry, go over it with a 1-inch barrel curling iron. Take 1-inch sections and alternate directions throughout by wrapping your hair around the wand.

"Break the curls up with your fingers to get a less sculpted look; it will make your hair look more beachy, more 'just tumbled out of bed.' Then finish with an anti-humidity hairspray to lock everything in.

"You don't want your style to look full and shellacked. Men like touchable hair that they can twine their fingers through, and there's nothing worse than when a guy puts his hands in your hair and it's stuck together with extensions or product."

ADVICE FOR MEN

"I have news for men that don't think their cut matters: style is definitely important. Not all styles are universal, though: you want something specific that suits your face shape and head shape. Guys don't have the added bonus of wearing makeup and may not be getting fit at the gym, which is why it's so important to see a professional and get a style that maximizes their potential.

"Product is a must. Gel is out -- wet looks aren't in anymore -- so I'd stick to texturizing products, pomades or pomade sticks. Most men don't spend a lot of money on their products, and to save money they're scrimping on conditioner without realizing how badly they need it. Most men don't realize that they need moisture in their hair no matter what; their scalps get dry and flakey and the ends look unhealthy. A good conditioner is a must and doesn't have to cost a lot.

"While styles change, there are certain looks that no man should ever wear. Fabio-length hair is an absolute no-no. Color for men is great but it's important to tread carefully with it. He doesn't want it look like a helmet. If he's covering grey, it's important to blend, blend, blend, because no woman thinks helmet head is sexy. Stick with shades in natural colors. There's nothing worse than a guy who goes to a pharmacy, buys Just For Men and comes out with a head full of uniform black hair.

"Chunky highlighted tips are also a no-no; those need to be retired forever. Men's hairstyling will always mimic female styles, so take a look at what women are playing around with in fashion magazines and ask your stylist for a male-friendly cut or color that apes the female look.

"Chemical straighteners also need to go, as does any look that is stemming from a teenage boy. A boyish look never translates well for a man; they should be looking to other men within their age groups for inspiration.

"There are so many lengths and styles that are in for a guy these days. Guys have options. He can have longer hair and will still look sophisticated, groomed and immaculate with the right cut and right products."

THE MALE OPINION:
KAZ AMOR, CELEBRITY STYLIST AT
WARREN-TRICOMI LA

"Men like shiny, healthy-looking, natural hair. Yes, we really *do* notice these things. We associate beautiful hair with a healthy lifestyle. We'll think that you take care of yourself, that you take pride in looking good.

"I'll tell you what we don't like: we hate over-processed hair. That doesn't mean that you can't use color – you can – just make sure the end result is healthy and shiny, because shine relates to the overall picture of health.

"Dull, crunchy and over-processed is a turn off. We don't like the feeling of dry or stiff hair.

When someone is kissing you, and her hair is touching you on your face or body, it feels good. It adds to the kiss.

"Have you ever noticed that men like to pet women? It's not because we're trying to treat you like a kid (as you think). If your hair is soft, we caress you because it feels good for us.

"Achieving this level of shine really has to do more with your general nutrition than with the products you use. If you eat crap foods, your hair is going to look like crap. If you eat a lot of foods with antioxidants, foods with olive oil or with vitamins B12 or B6, your hair probably looks great.

"If you want to know exactly what your body is lacking, you can take a hair sample to a nutritionist and they can tell you what vitamins you need.

"In terms of the products you should use to achieve this look, look for something that doesn't have parabens or preservatives. Shine products only work to seal in shine and protect against heat, but don't get to the root of the problem. They can also make your hair look greasy if you use too much.

"As a stylist, I try to achieve looks for my female clients that men like. I try to make women look natural and gorgeous."

"Men will say that they like no makeup at all, but what they really mean is that they like a neutral palette. These are two very different things. Men like glossy lips, mascara and rosy cheeks. They like all feminine features enhanced. They like long lashes, because you flirt with your eyes. They like glossy lips so they can imagine kissing you.

"Warning here though: now is not the time to break out new makeup trends, even if you happen to be a high fashion person. Your profile picture shouldn't reflect recent culture trends. You want to be yourself, but enhanced. I will say this, though: you need to be true to who you are. If you wear red lipstick or winged black eyeliner every single day, wear it in your profile picture. You want to represent who you really are. If you have a signature look, rock it, because the right person for you has to appreciate that."

FOUNDATION

"You want your skin to be even and have some sort of radiance to it. You're going to need foundation that has a luminous finish because men like a glow and that fresh, healthy look. Take a quarter-size amount and rub it between your fingers and press into your skin. By using your fingers, you're going to create that second skin look. Your look will look flawless, but you won't look like you have makeup on. Men want to see flawless, glowing skin; they don't want to see a mask.

TRY: Armani Luminous Silk foundation is the gold standard in terms of foundations, or MAC's Face & Body.

POWDER

"If you have a shiny complexion, it's only going to get picked up and amplified in photographs, so you're going to need to powder your face. You don't want to look matte or cakey; you want to keep up with the luminous, glowing finish look. Go for a powder which will set your makeup and gets rid of shine without mattifying the face. You want to go very light on the powder though; the whole point is to look a bit dewy.

TRY: Makeup Forever HD Microfinish Powder. Every makeup artist has it in their kit.

CHEEKS

"You want to mimic your own natural flushed shade when you're going for a blush. If you're cool (blue undertones) go for a pinkish color, while warmer skin tones (yellow undertones) should opt for peach. Here's an easy way to tell what shade you are: go out in the cold or go for a run and look at the color that's naturally appeared: that's what you want to mimic.

"You want to start by applying the color at the apples of your cheeks and blending upwards toward the temples. If you only do the apples, you might look clownish or too girlish. Blending up gives you a sultry look. There are three options here in terms of what kind of blush you should be using: I'd go for a creamer, liquid or light dusting of powder. If you have oily skin, opt for powder, but know that a cream or liquid looks the most natural. You'll look lit from within if you put cream blush on after foundation and before powder. To apply, tap your fingers into the pot and blend up.

TRY: Josie Maran cream blushes. They come in three shades only so it's easy to find your color, or Sue Devitt's Microquatic gel-to-powder blush.

HIGHLIGHTER

"Highlighter is great. You don't want to look like a Kardashian in your profile picture, but highlighter will help your cause. Apply it on the bridge of your nose, cheek bones and Cupid's bow. It will bounce back light from the flash in a way that not only brings your features forward in a way that men love, but also brightens and sculpts the face. The key here is that you don't want anything too metallic or shimmery for highlighter.

TRY: Josie Maran's Argan Illuminizer. I live for it. It's a super natural champagne shade and just a beautiful highlighter. People send me thank you notes saying that it changed their lives after they use it. Benefit's Moonbeam and Highbeam are also great options.

LIPS

"When you're doing your lips for you picture, you want to choose a nude shade like peach or pink, something natural looking. You also want to totally avoid lip liner. Men hate it, especially when it's visible. Go for a glossy look as opposed to something matte, because even though it might remind you of old Hollywood glamour, most men are scared by it as it's neither kissable or enticing. Finish with a gloss at the center of your mouth for fullness and dimension, which is what I do for the Victoria's Secret fashion show models; it adds to their pouts. Again, avoid the shimmery and sparkling stuff; you want a soft, creamy gloss.

TRY: Nars' Barbarella; it's a great peach or Nars Chelsea Girl Lip Lacquer. I get hit on every time I wear MAC's Boy Bait and Smashbox's Lip Enhancing Glosses are good because they have as light plumper for those who want slightly fuller lips.

EYELINER

"You're going for the natural look here, so you're not going to want to play up your eyes too heavily, but I do think you should go for a smudged eyeliner. Pencil works best. Harsh, precise lines don't look soft enough, nor do liquid or gel liners. Instead of going for a harsh, intense black pencil, choose a soft grey or brown. When smudged, they have a more alluring appeal.

TRY: Urban Decay's 24/7 Glide On Pencil or Estee Lauder's Stay in Place eye pencils, which have built in smudgers.

MASCARA

"When it comes to lashes, fuller is better…so coat them up! Lashes can be flirty. You want fullness, though you shouldn't have fake lashes on unless you wear them every single day, because it's false advertising. Amp up the mascara instead."

TRY: YSL Faux Cils for length and volume or Estee Lauder's Sumptuous. Great drugstore brands include L'Oreal's Voluminous – the original formula – and Cover Girl's Lash Blast.

EYESHADOW

"Go for a neutral palette when you're choosing your eye shadow; that's browns and flesh tones. You don't want a dark smoky eye. While you're applying your eye shadow, remember to fill in your brows. Nothing looks stranger than a face full of makeup with a naked brow."

TRY: MAC's Omega, Kid, Shroom, Brule or Cork.

SUE DEVITT, INTERNATIONAL MAKEUP ARTIST & FORMULATOR

"Look rejuvenated by applying a peach-tone concealer to the under-eye area. Apply with your fingertips from underneath your bottom lashes outward toward the temple. Then, lightly sweep powder over the top to set the look."

TRY: Bermuda Triangle Undereye Corrector, which counteracts the green and blue tones of dark circles with its smooth, peach-toned texture.

"For a perfect pout, try my buffing technique. 'Buff' the lips with a Lip Intensifier Pencil, applying the pencil with light feathering strokes around the lip line and blending inwards towards the center. Then, apply a matte or sheer lipstick evenly all over lips with a lip brush. This delivers maximum pigment and long-lasting color. Finally, finish with a lipgloss in sun-kissed pink or bronze to give your lips instant radiance."

"Primer may not be the first product you think about when applying makeup, but it makes a world of difference. A treatment primer applied before your foundation creates a smooth canvas for makeup application and actually helps bind makeup to the skin for longer wear throughout an entire day. When it comes to application, I've found the best way to apply foundation is with your fingertips. I do this with all my celebrity clients. Your hands allow you to really work around the different contours of the face, and most importantly allows you to feel your skin's hydration level. Start with the T-zone and work your way outward. Then, apply a light dusting of loose powder on the T-zone and cheeks, followed by concealer where needed."

"To make eyes really stand out, use rich, deep shades that complement and intensify your own natural eye color. Stay away from dull or flat tones, and experiment with rich eye shadow colors in jewel tones. For brown eyes, I suggest Eye Intensifier Pencil in Tanzania and Kenya; for blue eyes Eye Intensifier Pencil in Zaire and Ava; and for green eyes try Eye Intensifier Pencil in Surat and Bangalore. With Eye Intensifier Pencils you can almost mix and match any shade. That's how I create dramatic eyes for the red carpet."

"The key to achieving a sun-kissed glow is to create depth through layering product. Begin by applying a bronzing powder to the face, paying special attention to the apples of the cheeks, chin and forehead. Next, apply a bronzing lotion such as Microquatic™ Tinted Body Moisturizer. This will help create the depth of a true tan. To achieve strong cheekbones, highlight with soft pink and peach tones applied high on the apples of the cheeks for a youthful look."

STACY LONDON, STYLIST & HOST OF TLC'S "WHAT NOT TO WEAR"

"When people are online dating, they focus on trying to be witty or how to best describe themselves, but they don't seem to realize that what you look like is an essential part of the experience.

"For women, the Jennifer Aniston rule holds true: a white T-shirt and great-fitting pair of jeans are what boys like best. James Perse is a great option for T's and tank tops. In terms of style, I'd opt for a V-neck, as it's the most universally flattering. That doesn't mean a cleavage-baring V-neck, by the way, it just means a simple V-neck.

"If you're going to do a full-length shot and going for that simple, casual look, I'd advise against wearing a heel over four inches tall. That says 'you can have sex with me and leave me' – or that you strip for money. Then again, that also depends on what you want from your prospective dates. If you're looking for a good time, then by all means, wear as little as possible. But if you're looking for something serious, go simple.

"I'd also advise against wearing anything overly dressy in your photo. There are, of course, exceptions to the rule. If you're at a fancy event and someone takes a great candid picture of you in an evening dress, that's great. Just don't do anything intentionally posed or provocative. In my opinion, the more real you look, the better.

"When it comes to accessories, my big rule of thumb is that you shouldn't ever use animals. I don't mean animal print, I mean that a photograph of a single girl with a cat is online dating death. Cut out the embellishments: you only want to wear clothes or accessories that support or enhance who you are, not distract. Don't use your photo as an opportunity to wear a zillion bangle bracelets; stay natural.

"My advice for men, first and foremost, is not to wear a Bill Cosby sweater. That's a wise move. Beyond that, women want men to look real. If guys look overly manicured, women are going to wonder if you take more time in the bathroom mirror than they do, which is never a good look. Women want men to look effortless, manly but not dirty.

"Whatever your look is, make sure it's authentic. You can be a plaid button-down, skinny jeans-wearing hipster from Williamsburg or Venice, and as long as the look feels organic and not artificial, it will work. If you're a guy who wears suits all the time and that's part of who you are, by all means, wear that in your profile picture.

"The bottom line is this: be who you are. Don't overdo the makeup or accessories or wear something too provocative or skin-baring. You want people to see you for the possibility of you; you don't want to be a complete and total fantasy. If you're presenting the real you – whether you're male or female – you're not setting people up for disappointment. You want to set expectations in a way that's appropriate so that when you meet someone face to face, they aren't surprised by what you really look like. You don't want to pull punches. The point is to be genuine in an artificial setting. My advice for both genders is to wear something that makes you feel beautiful, confident and happy – because that does come across in your photographs.

"For a lot of people, there isn't any other way to meet a partner. Yes, it can be scary, but in another way, it brings the world to you. There are seven billion people on the planet, and you're not going to trip over them if you're not putting yourself out there somehow."

PART III:

TIPS FOR GOING ON YOUR FIRST DATE + WHAT TO DO IF YOU REALLY LIKE YOUR MATCH

CHAPTER 10:

TIPS FOR GOING ON YOUR FIRST ONLINE DATE

If you thought the hard part was over by finally agreeing to go out with a complete stranger, I've got news for you – you're only just beginning, baby. Going on the actual date is far more intimidating than simply speaking to a stranger via your computer. You have a whole new set of hoops to jump through. By the way, that isn't meant to put you off trying it out. Be bold! Live dangerously!

Before you psych yourself out of it, here's what you should know before you go:

Be safe

Your personal safety is the biggest concern you should have when online dating. Women in particular need to take extra precautions to in order to avoid online predators.

One of the best safety measures is to operate on the buddy system. Pick a wingwoman who will devote herself to coming to your rescue, should you need it. Instead of just vocalizing where you're going, send your friend the details in a text message, including the time and location of your date, as well as his online profile name and what site you met him on. That way, *should* something happen, she automatically has all the necessary information to track you down.

You'll also find the need for a good wingwoman should the date go badly. You might need saving if the guy is as boring as a piece of toast without butter or if he's getting too handsy for your liking. If you don't want to hurt his feelings, excuse yourself, take a bathroom break and text your lifeline to make that "emergency call." When she rings five minutes later, you can excuse yourself saying that work needs you or that there's something wrong with the cat you don't actually own. You'll be free as a bird, and even though he might suspect that you're lying, he has no proof and therefore cannot hate you for getting out of an awkward first date.

Conversely, if the guy who's asked you out doesn't show up and you're stuck at your meeting spot alone, make sure you're walking home in a brightly lit area. Take a cab if you have to; you never know whether or not the guy that stood you up did, in fact, come to the designated meeting spot in order to covertly follow you home. Take every security measure that you can.

How to escape a terrible date

When you're going on an online date and you haven't met the person in question, your odds are always 50/50. Will you get along? Will she bore you to tears? Will he actually look like his photographs or will he actually look like the human version of Alf?

These situations all sound pretty dire, but they can be easily prevented, even if you don't have an available friend to provide you with backup. As it happens, technology is good for a thing or two these days.

You're going to be saying "Hallelujah for the Smartphone!" if you ever need to get yourself out of an awful online date. The apps that exist these days can actually come to your rescue if you're stuck on a date with a dud.

The best of the bunch is called "Fake-Call Me." Not only can you choose the time for your faux call with this app, but it also allows you to say who the call is from. You have the option of choosing a specific ringtone and vibration, which would make an emergency call from your "mom" that much more legitimate. However, though a parental unit is a legitimate excuse to leave, if Brad Pitt shows up on your Smartphone screen, your date probably isn't going to buy what you're selling. In fact, if he or she believes that a celebrity is calling you in the first place, you're never going to get rid of your nosy date (especially if you live in LA and they happen to be a struggling actor/filmmaker/screenwriter).

"Phone My Phone" is another useful app to have, though it isn't as remarkable as "Fake-Call Me." It allows you to sign up for an "alarm" call. Beep! Your date is done; it's time to say sayonara. Do keep in mind that you only get ten free calls before you have to start paying for the service though.

A similar text-only tool is "Rescu'd." To use the service, save a number to your phone and type in when you want to be contacted. Like "Fake-Call Me," you have the option of customizing the call that comes in instead of getting a standard default message.

You'll have to hop on to your Twitter page for help if you want to use "Escape My Date." When you sign up for the site, you pre-select pals to call should you need to extract yourself from an uncomfortable situation. Then, when you've had enough of your not-so-great date, you send a direct message to the site's Twitter account, which then dispatches direct messages to your friends. If your buddies aren't as Tweet-happy as you are, the site will use Twilio to automate the phone call after five minutes. You can then make a run for it without hurting your date's feelings.

"GetMooh" is yet another option, and quite possibly the best if you're in desperate need of a laugh – which might be preferable to crying should you need to use "GetMooh" in the first place. The site rings you out of your mission impossible-to-go-on-with and allows you to pre-select your savior voice of choice. The options are endless. You can hear some sage words of advice from a psychic, a CIA agent, or even Alec Baldwin ranting at his "rude little pig" of a daughter. You can also record your own personalized message. Picture it now: "Dear future me, If you are hearing this message, you're clearly having a terrible time. It's time to extract yourself immediately and go home to have a tequila shot/pint of ice cream. By the way, kudos to you for being such a smart cookie! You can pat yourself on the back later, though. Right now it's time to makes moves. Pretend to look distressed about leaving right...about...*now*. Oh, by the way, did I forget to mention how much you love you right now?"

How to avoid awkwardness

Meeting up in person for the first time is as nerve-wracking for you as it is for your date. Although 1 in 5 people try online dating these days, there's still a stigma attached to saying you're going out with someone you met online.

There are ways of avoiding this embarrassment, of course. You can wait for your date outside the chosen meeting spot in order to walk in together. That way you won't have the restaurant/bar employees uncomfortably watching your every move in amusement throughout the course of the evening.

If the other person is already seated and you have a vague idea of what he or she looks like, act as if you've met the person before. Instead of saying, "Eric? Is that you? It's so nice to meet you!" be cool. Breeze on over and say, "Hey, what's up Eric?" This is effective at cutting the ice as well, because you're already pretending to be comfortable with that person, which, in turn, might actually make both of you *feel* more comfortable. If you've been emailing with any sort of frequency, you should feel that you've gotten to know each other a bit anyway. It's not as if you're complete strangers (just virtual ones).

What to wear

Chances are that, if you're going on a first online date, the place is going to be casual, well lit and informal. This means: no fancy dresses, no bling and no blazers.

Ladies, there is nothing hotter on *any* date, be it online or otherwise, than perfectly fitted blue jeans, a white T-shirt and heels or boots (though not the stripper kind, obviously). You'll look casual, sexy and as if you're not trying too hard. If the spot you're headed to is more of a lounge and less of a dive bar, opt for a statement necklace or a cocktail ring to make the outfit a little dressier. Hot tip: make the T-shirt a V-neck, and you're so money baby you don't even know it.

Guys, follow suit – though not *in* a suit. A simple T-shirt (aka nothing that says "Stussy," "Billabong" or "Hurley" with great jeans and trendy sneakers works, as does a T-shirt with tailored pants and nice shoes. There's no need to wear a tie or blazer though. You don't want to look like a stiff.

Who pays?

If I had a fortune cookie to answer this question, it would read: "He who asks for date must pay." And there you have it. Ladies, as you should never be pursuing a man in the first place (he may think you're easy if you do much more than wink at him to initiate contact) it's up to your companion to act like a gentleman.

However (ah yes, there's always a but isn't there?) if you're having an awful time or you want to bail early, don't force the poor guy to pay for you. If you're having one drink and you know you're never going to see him again, throw down a ten, make like a tree and leave. You'll feel better about yourself in the long run.

How long do you have to stay?

There's no exact rule of thumb for a first online date, but as it will most likely consist of a drink or coffee, you should leave yourself about an hour and a half; two if you're feeling really optimistic. A first online date is, in actuality, a pre-screening for a first date. You need to see if the banter you have online translates into real-life chemistry.

You also need to see if the person has lied about their physical appearance or if their smooth writing skills covered up their complete and utter social ineptitude. If they have, you're going to want to hightail it out of there.

To be on the safe side, stay no longer than an hour. If you're enjoying yourself, or still aren't sure whether or not you click, linger for ninety minutes. And if you're having a grand old time, heck, let the date go for three hours! But that's almost unheard of, so don't get your hopes up.

Where to go? / What to do?

I cannot stress this enough: never agree to dinner. You want to make that first date quick, painless and stress-free, so head to a coffee shop or a bar that's in a safe public place. Leave meals of any kind, or fun, quirky dates like an evening of mini-golf or an interactive bowling bar, for later on in the relationship. A fun and *cheap* date that every girl and guy can get behind is a frozen yogurt outing. There you have endless possibilities: inside or outside dining, a quick half hour meeting if the other person isn't quite your cup of tea or 90 minutes of fantastic conversation over your now-empty cups of fro-yo. This is a date that certainly won't break the bank, plus, if your companion sucks, at least you got *something* sweet out of the situation.

Can you kiss?

I'm sorry ladies and gents, but I do have a bit of a double standard here. If a woman is enjoying herself, she should feel free to give her date a goodnight kiss. I'm not talking sloppy, drunken make-out action here, and I'd advise you against using tongue, but a kiss is OK. It's better than a handshake. Guys, you need to be a little more restrained. Women already suspect that some of you are using online dating as a way of getting into their pants in the first place, so, if you want to see them again, you need to be on your best behavior. Don't go groping. Instead, smile, say you had a great time and then cut out gracefully. She'll not only be wondering why you didn't kiss her, but she'll start actually start wishing you had.

Can you go home with him?

If this is actually still a question for you, perhaps you need to re-read the previous paragraph a few hundred times until it's drilled into your head. You should be on your best behavior during these first dates – and that does *not* including showing him the time of his life. One study revealed that one in three women *do* sleep with a man on their first online date.[14] What the study *didn't* reveal is how many men ever call their promiscuous date again, but I imagine that very same one of three is waiting by their cell wondering, "Why didn't he call yet?" Um, duh. The same rings true for both online and offline dating: if you give it up right away, you're not only*not* presenting a challenge, but he'll probably think you're easy, too. I'm not setting women's lib back 100 years here or anything, I'm just stating a fact. Be as sexually adventurous as you please, just don't come crying if he isn't blowing up your phone.

Now that we've chatted about having the morals of an alley cat, you need to remember that

••••••••••••••••••••••••
14   *Grant, Alexis.* August 20, 2007. <http://www.chron.com/news/houston-texas/article/1-in-3-female-online-daters-report-first-date-sex-1528231.php?plckFindCommentKey=CommentKey:c8e52b29-7e5a-451b-b8dd-b16b7dbad916 >.

you're going home with a complete stranger. He could very well be lying about his identity or try something against your will if you're entering his lair in the name of being young, having fun and getting your rocks off. You need to know that you could be making the dumbest decision of your life.

BARRY'S STORY: BEWARE THE CRAZIES (AND NYMPHOMANIACS) YOU MIGHT MEET ONLINE

"I went on one date with this girl I met on JDate, and she literally went nuts. The date was OK, really nothing special. I didn't think I wanted to see her again, but she solidified that sentiment with her behavior.

"A few days after our date, she called me, furious that she hadn't heard from me. I took the manly approach and outright told her – honestly – that I wasn't interested in seeing her again.

"She spent the next 1½ hours trying to convince me that I was wrong and listed the reasons why I should date her. I'm not sure why I lingered on that phone call for so long, but by the end of it, when I held my ground and didn't budge, I thought it would all be over. But it wasn't – not by a long shot.

"A few months later I got yet another call from Shira that I didn't pick up, saying that she was near my house and wanted to see me. Ignore, abort. A few months after *that* she called me yet again and, when I didn't pick up, left a voicemail.

"It was the most desperate voicemail I have ever heard in my life. She admitted that she had blocked her number in the hopes that I'd pick up if I knew it wasn't her. She said that she thought she'd take another route because she assumed I just wasn't ready for a relationship. She thought because I didn't want to be with her, that meant I wasn't ready – which is so far from the truth it isn't even funny.

"But then she offered herself to me on a platter because she 'thought that was what I wanted'. She propositioned a no-strings attached sleepover. She even offered to come and pick me up. Luckily, the message cut her off. I had heard the whole thing and knew it was her, so when she called back, I picked up.

"I knew it was harsh, but what I basically told her was, 'I'm not interested. Please understand, and leave me alone.' She was totally disrespecting herself.

"What it basically comes down to is that she saw something in me that she didn't see in others. For some reason, she had decided that I was the one she desired for a partner. When she was denied, she took what she thought was the only available route for me to consider her as an option. Unfortunately, she didn't ask anyone else if they thought this was a good idea."

JON'S PLEA:
LADIES, SHOWING A LITTLE RESPECT
ISN'T SO HARD TO DO

"Online dating requires so much time, energy and money from a man, that I really just wish a girl would let me know if she wasn't interested. It's not that hard, and it doesn't require much effort to be nice.

"I've been using matchmaking sites for years as a way of meeting people that I might not have met otherwise, though I also meet girls in the more traditional ways – out at night, through friends, through work. No matter how I'm meeting a woman, I always try to be respectful and to be a gentleman, even though that same level of respect isn't always reciprocated.

"Guys needs to spend a lot of time making their emails original and funny, and to be honest, more often than not they're not even going to get read. Women are going to read it long enough to delete it or not at all if you don't have whatever their fantasy picture is. For girls, it's like skimming through annoying junk mail, though they did, in fact, sign up and pay for the site.

"Ladies, please, just tell me you're not interested. I'd prefer that to not receiving a response to my thoughtful email at all. I bet you're wondering why would I prefer that a girl tell me she wasn't interested. Why would I want to be rejected, right? Part of it is that I'm expected to make the initial move and I have to put myself out there, so why shouldn't they show me a common courtesy by responding?

"Online dating is essentially just a bunch of people who have agreed to play by a certain set of rules in order to meet someone, but that doesn't mean you don't have to be polite when you play the game.

"If a girl I'm not interested in writes to me, I always write her back to tell her – very nicely – that I'm not into it. I always wish her luck on finding a man that fits what she's looking for.

"As for going on actual dates, it can be an expensive business for a guy. I generally always pay, which is why going on four billion dates a week is both costly and disheartening, so I try to get to know a girl first, and after about a week of chatting online, I ask her out. Here's my rule of thumb: if you ask them to meet you, you should suck it up and pay.

"I've also started to view that first date not so much as a date, but as an interview. I'm slower to the punch when treating that first meeting like an actual date. I'm not trying to get a good night kiss – I'm actually just trying to get to the second date so we can start from there.

"I went out with this one girl I met on Match, and it was almost like a timer went off in the middle of the date. She was in the middle of responding to something I had just been talking about, and all of a sudden she said, 'Well, this has been nice,' got up and left.

"That's the thing about online dating. People aren't just looking for someone they can have an OK time with. It's much more specific than regular dating because you're actually listing the criteria for what you want from the get-go. In real life, I'd probably give people more of a chance if I had a non-offensive but boring first date. If there wasn't anything that screamed 'This girl is awesome!' I'd probably still go on another date. But on a dating site, if you don't really hit it off right away, you know it's not going to work out and you won't be going on a second date.

"Back to that mutual respect I was talking about. If women were just honest, that would be great. If you don't want me to call you, tell me. This might seem counterintuitive because it doesn't happen a lot, but the fact of the matter is that most relationships don't work. The ones that do -- good relationships -- are based on the fact that people know how to communicate with each other. It's less awkward then ignoring phone calls and wondering when he's going to finally get the hint and stop."

CHAPTER 11:

THE WORST ONLINE DATES OF ALL TIME

If you've ever been on a bad date (as I'm sure you all have), you'll know how painful it can be. Trust me, your experiences aren't half as bad as what these online daters have suffered. Something tells me you're going to finish reading these stories, breathe a sigh of relief, grab a shot of tequila, look upward and say, "Bottoms up, Big Guy. Just thanking my lucky stars right now."

To all those scarred by the following online dates, I salute you for having the strength to get through them.

EDWARD'S STORY:
WHY ONE DATE TURNED ME OFF
ONLINE DATING FOREVER

"I was lonely, so I decided to put myself out there and join Match. I took twenty minutes to fill out the questionnaire and put a normal profile picture up, nothing fancy. With me, what you see is what you get. Unfortunately, I was getting people who didn't fit what I was looking for. I was getting younger, older, taller, but not what I wanted.

"So when this blonde contacted me and wanted to meet up, I thought, 'Why not?' Her photos were a little bit glammed up and I could tell she had put herself out there at her peak; but I went anyway.

"We decided to meet at Jerry's Deli in LA. I was there on time and waited for her for an hour. She had actually been there the entire time but let me sit there at the bar just looking around to see if she'd show.

"Eventually she came up to me and introduced herself. She told me right away that she had been there the entire time and 'wanted to see what I would do.' I already knew it was going to be a bad night.

"Adding to that weirdness, she looked nothing like her picture. Apparently she didn't think I'd recognize the difference between a blonde and a brunette. In her photo, she had this very long, very blonde hair. In person, her hair was brown, super short, curly and up around her ears. I knew she was a little off, but I still acted like a gentleman.

"We chitchatted and I told her what I did for a job; I was working as a freelance photographer

137

and a camera store manager at the time. I made a decent living, I had nothing to be ashamed of.

"But she started in with all these weird questions, like did I own property and did I have any kids. They were particularly odd questions for a first date given that we had met on an online dating site and I had already answered all those questions in my questionnaire. I felt like I was being checked for my credit score rather than compatibility.

"But the evening got worse, if at all possible. She has a Cosmopolitan – one of those drinks *Sex and the City* made popular for sophisticated single girls – and obviously didn't like that I chose to drink a beer. I was being judged on everything. In one of her messages, she had told me to come to the date dressed in jeans; she said 'come casual.' But she was there looking all dressed up and was disdainful about my jeans and sneakers, as if I were in the wrong. I was clearly out for display.

"So, I was there in my awful clothes and with my not-up-to-par job, but this girl who had lied about what she looked like refused to say what *she* did for a living. Her vague answer was that she 'hung around.' I'll just be she did. Hung around looking for rich guys on Match, more like.

"Twenty minutes later I was just done, I was ready to go. I didn't have the heart to tell her it wasn't working out, so I just suffered through her demanding to know why, as a 30-something man,

I didn't own my own house and other criticisms of the way I chose to live my life.

"The last thing she said to me was, 'You don't have a house and you don't drive a nice car.' She then took a sip of her Cosmopolitan and said, 'Excuse me, I need to go to the ladies room.' But she didn't go to the restroom. She just left – and left me to pay for her drink.

"The bartender just looked at me incredulously and was like, 'What in the heck was that?' I told him, 'I really hope she doesn't call me again.' She didn't, but I still consider that to be a $49 date, because after that atrocity, I never used Match again. I deleted my account and just gave up. I haven't been on an online date since.'

BETTE'S STORY:
HE PULLED THE OLD
'I FORGOT MY WALLET TRICK'

"I had just moved to Los Angeles at the age of 23 and I wanted to meet new people, so I joined eHarmony. Mind you, this was my first online date ever, so I didn't know what tricks people could play; I took things at face value.

"Bob and I met online, talked for a bit and then set up a day and time to meet and go to dinner. He asked me to meet him at his house, which, in hindsight, should have been my first red flag.

"When I got to his house, he invited me in for a glass of wine. He sat on his couch the entire time quite literally making out with his dog while carrying on a conversation with me. "Stella" was kissing him on the mouth and he really seemed to like it. All I could think was 'awkward.'

"He told me he had made reservations at this nice bistro – which also happened to be the name of his dog (he *really* liked that dog!) at 6:30. He drove and we arrived at the restaurant right on time. As we valeted the car he 'pretended' to go for his wallet. I didn't realize he was faking it at the time. 'Oh my God, I forgot my wallet!' he said – and then *walked around the car* to my side, opened my door, reached over me and grabbed his *passport* out of the glove compartment. 'That's a relief,' he said. 'I have my passport, so at least I can drink.'

"When I started to say that we could go back to the house and get his wallet, he was adamant that we stay. He said, very firmly, that we had a reservation and that they wouldn't take us later and we needed to go in. He said, 'Do you mind paying? I'll get you back when we get to the house.' At that point I really thought he might.

"Inside was a nightmare. It was the typical scenario of a girl going out with a guy just because he's paying -- and totally taking advantage of the fact – flipped. Bob ordered an expensive bottle of wine. He ordered one of the most expensive beef entrees on the menu, which was around $40. He insisted on an appetizer, dessert, the whole shebang.

"To make matters worse, we had absolutely nothing in common at all. It was a disaster. He kept talking and eating and I kept wishing he would shut up so that we could leave.

"Eventually he finished, I paid and we drove back to his house. So literally, as soon as we got back, I said, 'I'm going home now' and lingered for a few seconds, hoping he'd man up and get me the money he had promised me, or at least his share of the meal. Yeah, that didn't happen.

"He said, 'OK, good night', got out of the car and walked away. I was only 23! I didn't know what to do! But my reaction then was the same one I have now: good riddance! I didn't want to deal with anymore. $150 and one horrible date later made me realize that I had made a very expensive mistake. But you better believe I learned my lesson."

LACEY'S STORY:
I WENT OUT WITH THE MOST
SELF-CENTERED MAN OF ALL TIME

"I met my fiancé through eHarmony, and although I love it for that reason, I still went on the most horrible date of my life through that site. We went to a wine bar, where you get a card and swipe for every pour that you want. Literally from the moment he arrived, my date talked about how horrible his job was. He was still talking about it an hour later. I was so bored at that point that I finally blurted out (when he paused for breath), 'If you hate your job so much, why don't you just look for another one?' I thought that would effectively end the discussion, but I had no such luck.

"He looked at me condescendingly and said, 'You just don't understand.' He then kept talking for another ninety minutes. I tried to talk about something else, but I totally got shut down. Eventually I said, 'Listen, you've been talking about this for two and a half hours now and I think you should seriously look for another job if you hate this one so much.' Then, I kid you not, he stood up, said, 'You have no empathy' and walked out! I stayed and finished my wine, thinking, 'Thank God he pre-paid for this.'

"I only agreed to go out with him in the first place because I thought I was being too picky and that eHarmony must have put us together for a reason. I still can't figure out what that reason is."

HAYLIE'S STORY: I WOUND UP GOING HOME...WITH THE COPS

"I met a guy from a nearby town on Match who was 24 years old and lived at home with his parents, which I was fine with. After a bit of chatting online, we decided to go on our first (and last) date. We met for dinner, but he hadn't made reservations and the wait was too long, so he offered to drive to a restaurant down the street.

"I was dressed nicely for the date, because it was a dinner thing. We were walking through the parking lot – me in heels – having a nice conversation when we stopped in front of a tow truck, which just so happened to be his vehicle. First, after climbing on up, my heel got stuck in the side step. Then, as it happened, it turned out he was actually still at work, on call for AAA! He had to do a lockout system for a guy who had left his keys in his car. All the while, I stuck it out with a smile on my face.

"We finally made it to dinner and I thought, 'OK, let's forget the first part of the date. Things will get better.' Except, they didn't. He ate like a five-year-old, shoving food in his face and dribbling all over his chin. It was beyond gross. An hour later I thought the nightmare was coming to an end and ready to go home and call it a night, but it turned out that the nightmare was only beginning.

"While he was driving me back to my car, my date got a call about a car crash so he switched directions, threw his tow lights on and took off his nice button-down shirt only to reveal that he was wearing a dirty, greasy, disgusting T-shirt under-neath. We make it to the accident scene and he gets out and does what he has to do to get the smashed up car on his truck. A lot of time has gone by, and he informs me that the 'date' is continuing, be-cause he has to take the car to the junkyard. I told him that I wanted to go home, but he insisted that he had to finish his job first.

"By then, I had had it. Without another word, I hopped out of his truck and the asked the police officer on the scene for a ride back to my car. The worst date of my life was finally over and I must admit that I'm a little battle scarred by it. At least it still made for a great topic at work the next day!"

CHAPTER 12:

WHEN TO BECOME EXCLUSIVE & DITCH THE DATING PROFILES

Sorry if this chapter title is misleading, because I've found that becoming exclusive with your online love and ditching your dating profile aren't mutually exclusive situations. Meaning: many people may have decided to date someone seriously, but leave their profiles up...just in case.

You can choose to look at this in one of two ways: you're already admitting defeat before actually giving the relationship a fair shot, or you can say you're just being practical. Glass half full here, friends: I'd go with the latter option.

It's going to make you feel like something the dog did if you've been on a handful of dates, really like the person you've been seeing and realize that their profile is not only up, but that they've been on it quite actively while you were actually starting to fall head over heels.

Online, like offline dating, is still a process. Just because you've had lengthy chats via your computer doesn't mean that you need to rush into a relationship straight away. I'm assuming you've all heard the expression 'You can't hurry love,' yes?

DO NOT take down your profile until you have 'the talk' about going exclusive. There's no big rush to take yourself off the market if your partner isn't in the same place.

Some people believe in "The Rules." You know what I'm talking about – no kissing until date two. No sex until date five. Don't contact him first. Blah, blah, blah, blah, blah. Sorry to say this, but if you're a real law-abiding citizen, you should know that there's an entirely new rulebook in effect when you're online dating. You don't magically become a couple after 15 dates. Just because he likes you doesn't mean he wants to be with *just* you.

That said, if you've been out with someone more than a handful of times, you should probably cut back on your online dating site usage. If he or she sees that you've been on your site of choice every single day, they might just assume that you're still looking for love with someone else.

Once you do become exclusive, for Pete's sake, take your profile down! You don't have to delete it completely. If you don't honestly believe the situation is going to work in the long run, then hide your profile; you can always put it back up again if the relationship doesn't work out. But when you agree to become "exclusive," you're making a promise to someone else – and there is no fine print addendum in "exclusive" that says you're allowed to date someone else.

Sites like HowAboutWe.com have a deactivate feature, which allows you to take your profile down without deleting it permanently. Should you and your partner call it quits, you can put your account back up in the same pristine manner in which you left it.

Just one tip here: if you've gone offline for any length of times, make sure to update your photographs. You want to depict yourself in the most honest way possible. I think we can all agree that liars suck.

KATHERINE'S STORY: HOW WE BECAME EXCLUSIVE

"My boyfriend Rob and I met on OKCupid around Thanksgiving 2010 and decided to become exclusive in January of 2011. We were already serious by the time we decided to close our accounts.

"We had been kidding about doing it, but then, one day, we actually decided to shut them down. It wasn't a big deal. It was pretty obvious how we felt about one another.

"But here's the thing. I was in Costa Rica for a month and for some reason I couldn't track down his number. I remembered that he had first given me his number on OKCupid, so I re-opened my account in order to call him.

"I now have my profile up because my best friend is on [the site] and she frequently wants me to look at some guy or another's profile if she's considering dating him. It's not like I'm going to respond if someone sends me a message.

"I think my boyfriend would prefer that I don't have it, but at least he knows about it; I wouldn't try to hide it from him. We've certainly never fought about it, but he does tease me about it quite a bit. I guess that's only fair."

PART V:

BEWARE — THERE ARE DOWNSIDES TO ONLINE DATING

CHAPTER 13:

FOR LOVE OR NOOKIE – WHAT GUYS ARE REALLY LOOKING FOR ONLINE

I'm going to drop a bombshell on you here, so prepare yourself. Are you ready? Men like sex. WOW. I'm sure you're slack-jawed right now by my revelation. Let's just say I gave you that one. You can thank me later.

Alright fine, you're not *really* surprised, are you? You do know what men want. I want you to keep that in mind especially when you're about to log on to your site of choice. You have to be hyper aware that there's a large percentage of men out there who see the online dating community as one big, virtual shopping mall that will help them in their quest to score with as many women as often as possible.

Just so we're on the same page here, I'm testing you to make sure you aren't totally naïve. There are some guys out there who join dating sites actually seeking a relationship, but you *do* know that there are men out there who will seduce you, never call, block your profile and then do it all over again to another unsuspecting female as well.

A recent study published in the journal *Sex Roles* [15] confirmed that, as a gender, men would almost always opt for casual sex on tap than to be in monogamous, yet loving, relationship. Researchers have "discovered" that, given a choice, men prefer to "hook up" (or what I prefer to call having "sexual shenanigans") rather than seriously date someone.

So how do you know what a guy is really after? The signs are usually pretty obvious, but just in case you were oblivious in the wake of his chiseled abs, pretty face and six-figure income, here are some red flags to keep you on your toes.

If his messages quickly veer into sexual territory or his flirtatiousness borders on being inappropriate, ditch him. If he says anything provocative, even the cheesy old "So, what are you wearing?" don't feel bad about blocking him and/or reporting him.

In fact, when you're first beginning to chat with someone online, sex shouldn't come up at all. Rule of thumb. A man who doesn't know you shouldn't be privileged enough to know what

15   *Agarwal, Kangna* . April 8 2010. <http://www.themedguru.com/node/33871>

your favorite position is, or what your craziest sexual experience was in the past. Your best friends may not even be privy to information that private – so why reveal all to a complete stranger?

Sometimes you won't be able to tell that he's a creeper until you actually go on a date. Say that after a series of harmless emails, you decide to meet in person for the first time. You're at a dimly lit bar, you're flirting, you're attracted to one another. He looks like his picture, doesn't seem to have anything seriously wrong with him, isn't wearing a wedding band and you haven't caught him flirting with the waitress yet. "This might work," you think to yourself.

But then, after your second glass of wine, he puts his hand on your knee. He leaves it there. His other hand creeps up to the back of your neck until you seriously begin to believe that he might be an octopus disguised as a handsome male human. He tries to plant one on you though you're out in public and seems a bit miffed when he's brutally rebuffed. He isn't upset for long though, nor does he give up in his pursuit.

Eight minutes later, when you've had to fend the human caterpillar off yet again, you decide to cut the date short. How were you to know he'd suddenly morph into handsy Harry? He seemed so *normal* online.   •

Although you can't control what your date does, you can control what *you* do. If you find yourself in a sticky situation, never feel that you have to give it the good old college try just because he's taken you out and paid for a few cocktails. You are never obligated to kiss, make out with or sleep with any man. If he's making you feel uncomfortable, cut the date short (you'll learn about some fool-proof escape tactics later) and get the hell out of there.

If he contacts you again – which he might if he wrongly thought he should have 'gotten' something (sexual) out of the evening – politely but firmly tell him via an email or message that you believe you'd be better off as friends. Keep it short and sweet. He may not appreciate your honesty, but that's life. Rejection is never pleasant.

Like I said before, not all guys are going online looking to get laid. Some are genuinely too busy to have a normal dating life. Businessmen living in large cities in particular are consumed by their high-pressure jobs. This is a prime example of the kind of man you might meet online: successful, physically fit and too tied to their job to meet many people out and about.

Then there are those that simply see the Internet as another dating tool at their disposal. Smart boys. Online dating *is* a brilliant way to meet someone you might not have met otherwise

-- if you're using it in the right way, for the right reasons, that is.

KELLY'S STORY:
A GUY ACTUALLY OFFERED
TO PAY ME FOR SEX

"You seriously never know who you're going to meet online. One night I was home and bored, and this guy messaged me on OKCupid. I couldn't really tell what he looked like – he had sunglasses on in his photos – but I didn't have anything else to do so I responded.

"We were having a normal conversation and had exchanged a few messages each when, out of the blue, he asked me if I would come over and have sex with him! Even worse, he then offered to pay me $2,400. He told me to come over and wear a kinky schoolgirl outfit.

"I stopped responding to him, but he sent me about twenty messages anyway which said increasingly sexual, awful things. I was totally freaked out, so I blocked him and then reported him. I was so grossed out by the whole situation; I felt so violated. There are definitely some creepy people online."

JON'S STORY:
I WAS LOOKING FOR A RELATIONSHIP

"I had a friend who met her husband on Match, so I decided that, despite my long-standing struggles with the concept of online dating, if someone that I respected and liked a lot as a person said it actually worked, then I'd say 'fair enough. I'll try it.'

"When I moved to Seattle, I didn't know anyone, so it also seemed like the appropriate thing to do. But I wasn't just dating online. It's one way of meeting people, but not an exclusive method.

"I have been out on a lot of dates, but of the first dates that I went on, there were only two girls that I thought I'd go out with again. In both cases, the dates ended up lasting for a few hours. If we enjoyed each other's company for more than a brief time, I'd take it as a sign that I should call them again.

"I was looking for a relationship, and I found one. I've been dating a girl that I met online for two and a half months and we're still going strong. Going on a matchmaking site looking to get laid has never even occurred to me."

CHAPTER 14:

HOW TO SPOT A PLAYER

Given the opportunity, most men aren't going to jump at the chance to hit the shops like a woman would. But then, buying a button-down can hardly offer the same kind of thrill that browsing for a beautiful woman can. Some men might be totally overwhelmed by their seemingly unlimited options, while others might think "I'd like that, and that, and that – so why just choose one?" This is why you need to be aware and beware of the online player.

Naturally, you don't want to date a dude that has five other girlfriends on the go. You want to be his one and only. So how can you spot a man who has wandering eyes and roving fingertips? Here are the signs…

♥ **His profile's been up since 1992**
OK, so maybe he hasn't been doing the online dating thing for twenty odd years, but he *hasn't* had success in quite some time. Or maybe he has – in the way that he wants, at

least. Perhaps he enjoys being chronically single, but you aren't going to enjoy being one of the many women he mingles with. Check and see just how long he's been a member, and if it's been over a year, don't respond.

♥ **It's a numbers game**
If his profile has attracted way more views than other male profiles, be wary. The more time per day you spend online, the more your profile is being seen. This means dudecakes is very "active" in the online dating community.

♥ **He doesn't want to meet you**
A guy who refuses to take your online relationship into the real world despite dozens of exchanged messages should raise a red flag. He craves your attention but isn't interested in getting to know you outside of his virtual world.

♥ **He's got "stalkers"**
Or so he tells you. The truth is most likely that the "stalkers" in questions are girls he's leading on (does that sound familiar?) that he likes to keep around to feed his ego.

♥ **He tells you he's never "felt this way before"**
The real question you want to ask yourself

is "does he feel anything at all?" A guy who pretends you're having a serious relationship online right away if you've only been chatting is taking you for a ride. Sorry, sister.

♥ **He matches your answers with his**
We ladies have a tendency to believe that things – and by things, I mean "relation-ships" – are fated. If you're having a hard time wrapping your head around just how much you have in common, take a step back and analyze the situation for what it is. Is he asking you questions and then matching his responses to yours? If you've answered in the affirmative here, you could be dealing with a frequent male shopper. This guy is a mas-ter playing the game, and you're letting him win. To catch an online player, try asking *him* the questions for once, and see if he actually responds with something that isn't totally vague. After all, two can play that game…

♥ **He hides his profile**
He does this to make you think he's gone off the dating market because you're "the one" for him, but in actuality, he's still using and abusing – you just can't see it.

♥ **He moves way too fast**
He meets you online and after two or three messages, he's immediately asked for your phone number and ready to move your all-too-brief relationship to the next level. Watch out! Never give your private information to a guy you can't be certain of.

DEBBIE'S STORY: HOW I GOT LUCKY AND AVOIDED AN ONLINE LOTHARIO

"I joined Match.com about two years ago, but was lucky enough to have a friend in the area who had been on the site for a while. There are a lot of stalkers and guys pretending to be someone they're not on there, and I wanted to avoid them at all costs. My friend would tell me about the jerks she had met and would warn me against them. Lo and behold, the exact men she warned me about did what she said they would, so I didn't have to waste my time going out with creeps when there were so many legitimately nice guys out there.

"There was one guy in particular she warned me against, but we had already been emailing. He moved quickly, that was for sure. I had only been on the site for a week and we had already set up a date! Anyway, after hearing what a creeper he was, I cancelled the date. The next day, I got a weird message confirming everything she had told me. He sent me this ranting email acting out all his insecurities. He wrote, 'You're rejecting me and you don't even know me. How can you do that? Why would you do that? Women are so weird. Women are awful. You're all the same.' In hindsight, you can't know just how glad I am that I listened to her!"

CHAPTER 15:

HOW TO SPOT A CHEATER

The Definition of Cheating

1: a: to practice fraud or trickery
   b: to violate rules dishonestly

2: to be sexually unfaithful – usually used with *on*

3: to position oneself defensively near a particular area in anticipation of a play in that area[16]

Although all above of the above definitions apply to cheaters, I tend to think #3 describes the married men looking for a quick fling online to a T. These toolbags have figured out to screw around without getting caught – and are also aware of which women are the most susceptible to buying their BS.

....
16 *Merriam Webster.* 2012. <http://www.merriam-webster.com/ dictionary/cheat>

161

Unfortunately, online dating sites *are* great places for two-timers to troll for women without getting caught – and it's a growing trend. Here's a scary but true fact: according to a MSNBC study[17], 30% of the men using online dating sites are actually married. THIRTY PERCENT. Even worse, the results of a DivorceMag study [18] revealed that only 46% of the men polled thought that online affairs should be constituted as cheating. Are these dudes high?!

It's time to weed out these bad, adulterous seeds and save yourself potential heartache. You'll find out to do so below, but before you read, I have one request: *if you know he's a cheater, report that mothertrucker.* Don't let him get away with it again by pulling one over a woman who isn't as savvy as you. Go buy yourself something nice as a reward – you'll deserve it.

He doesn't have a profile photo

Most married men know better than to post a photograph of themselves online, though they *will* email you one if you ask. It's too risky to plaster

17 *Weaver, Jane.* 2007. <http://www.msnbc.msn.com/id/17951664/ ns/health-sexual_health/t/many-cheat-thrill-more-stay-true-love/#.Tzc2S10zL6k   http://www.onlinedatingsafetytips.com/ MarriedMenandCheaters.cfm>

18 *Meyer, Cathy.* 2012. <http://divorcesupport.about.com/od/ emotionalaffairs/f/onlineaffairs.htm>

their picture all over any sort of dating site lest one of their wives' friends or relatives happens to be secretly on the site as well.

He only emails you from a generic account

If he persists in emailing you from an account that also conveniently happens to be a variation of his online screen name, you might be smelling a rat. If he never emails you from his work account or from something more personal -- as most of us have Gmail accounts using our first and last names – then beware: he's hiding something.

He won't tell you his last name

Warning bells should be going off if you've been out more than a handful of times with this guy and he's still hesitant about letting you know exactly who he is. It's fine to be wary on the first date, and quite possibly even the second, but after spending a fair bit of time with him, you should have a better sense of who he is.

He has a pattern

If you notice that he's a) only online during certain times of the day b) contacting you at a specific hour every day or c) only wants to see you during a very specific set of hours, then something is definitely up. He's trying to fit you in where you won't conflict or cause problems in his real life – or with his wife.

Phone unfriendly

Has he refused to give you his number and still persists in corresponding via email or the dating site you met on? Has he given you his number, but it goes straight to voicemail every time you try to call him? Have you ever been in the midst of a great phone conversation where he hangs up out of the blue and then texts you that he had a work emergency or lost the connection? If any of these scenarios sound familiar, watch out – he doesn't want his respective other to catch him in the act.

He's using a free dating site

Though cheaters aren't *just* using free sites like OKCupid, they do tend to opt for non-paying options, especially if they're married. A cheater doesn't plan on getting caught, and the last thing he wants is the bill for a matchmaking site appearing on his monthly credit card statement. A two-timer is going to try his best to play smart while he's playing you.

He's lied in the past

When you're trying to get to know someone, you want to know everything about them, so of course you're listening intently when he speaks. If anything in his story switches during the initial stages of your relationship, you might want to beware: a man who lies about one thing may be lying about many more. To note here: he'll flip the situation on you and make it seem like *you* were the one who misunderstood or got confused. Only, you didn't: he's trying to cover up very nearly getting caught.

He always suggests going back to your place

If you've been dating someone for more than a few months and he never once offers to let you see his place, but is hell-bent on spending as much time in your neck of the woods as possible instead, it's time to get skeptical. A guy who never introduces you to his world is doing so because it's a world in to which you're not welcome.

He consistently cancels plans

If something is "always coming up" when you have any sort of plans – be it dinner, a weekend away in the country or just a day hanging out by your pool – something is going on, and it *isn't* his demanding boss constantly calling as he says.

Don't ignore your intuition

If your gut tells you something is fishy, listen. You're wiser than you know.

FREYA'S STORY: HE WAS MARRIED

"I was new to online dating so I joined Match.com about five years ago. I met this guy who called himself Blue Eyed Romeo. I should have realized that something was up, because he always wanted to grab 'a bite' between the hours of 3 and 6 pm.

"We went on four dates total and I never even kissed him, because deep down I knew something was wrong. I mean, at first I chalked it up to the weirdness of online dating, but then as things progressed I began to realize that I wasn't dealing with a normal situation.

"Romeo owned a bar about an hour away from he lived in Southern California. The place was real; I had even been there before.

"He had always contacted me in the past, but I hadn't heard from him for a few days and I suddenly had the urge to talk to him, so I called. A woman answered the phone. I was as confused as she sounded when I asked, 'Hi. Is Johnny there?' I could hear the suspicion dripping in her voice when she said, 'Yes, he is. Who is this?'

"At that point, I was steaming. I realized what was happening, and I think she did as well. So Johnny gets on the phone and literally has the nerve to say, 'Thanks so much for calling back. No, the waitressing position has been filled. If anything opens up, we'll let you know.'

"It was obviously his live-in girlfriend or wife. He was totally using Match to cheat! Beware of who you're meeting online; they may not be exactly who they say they are."

CHAPTER 16:

HOW TO SPOT A CRIMINAL

As I'm sure you're all aware of by now, there are definitely downsides to online dating, just as there are to meeting a partner offline. In addition to worrying about cheaters, liars and players, you also have to also protect yourself against the men that are *really* dangerous: online predators.

There really is a big cause for concern here. One out of every ten sex offenders use online dating sites to prey on women.[19] But don't let that scare you off. You'll just have to be extra smart about your dating choices from now on.

One way to completely avoid this issue is to join a site that does background checks, like True. com.

True's President Ruben Buell, has promised that the site has investigated every single one of its subscribing members since its 2003 launch.

"We wanted to change the way dating sites were perceived and the way people used them

19 *Relationshiplab.* 2010. http://relationshiplaboratory.com/
latest-research-online-dating-statistics-revealed/

so that when someone came online, they had a much better understanding that the person they were talking to was not a convicted felon," he explained. [20]

Hallelujah!

Seriously, you need to watch out. If you're dismissing this section already and saying to yourself, "Well, *duh*. I think I would know if I was talking to a felon" sorry, but you're wrong.

Even the big daddy of dating sites, Match. com, has its epic fails. A San Antonio man, who happened to be a convicted murderer, was trolling for dates on the matchmaking site until a local paper revealed his shady past.

Match took down Abraham Fortune's profile as a way of minimizing the backlash that ensued, but the damage was done. Fortune's presence online alone should be enough to tell you that you need to be vigilant about who you're meeting and how much you're revealing about yourself to a complete stranger.

In addition to looking for a site that does background checks like True, you may want to bite the bullet and join a paying site if you're serious about looking for love online. Sure, the beauty of sites like OKCupid is that they're free, but that also means that anyone can join.

•••••••••••••••••••••••
20 *Heussner, Ki Mae.* July 1, 2010. <http://abcnews.go.com/Technology/online-dating-sites-background-checks/story?id=11063166#.TznCxMozL6l>.

A scam artist/predator would be more inclined to go the way of the Craigslist personal ads then slap down his credit card (if he even has one), but then again, you never know who's really sitting behind the other computer.

You also want to check if the site you're thinking about joining is a member of the Better Business Bureau.[21] The BBB can how many complaints have been filed against a particular service, as well as why the complaint has been filed.

ConsumerAffair.com [22] is another massive database that logs user grievances. If you're taking the time to actually look on one of these security sites, be thorough. Make sure you read every bitch and moan instead of simply skimming through quickly.

The most important thing I can tell you is here to *use common sense*. When you start chatting up a guy online, never, ever give him your full name or phone number right away. If he has access to those two very important things, what's going to prevent him from digging up more dirt online? Much of our personal information is on the Internet these days, and it won't take much sleuthing to pull up your Facebook profile, Twitter account or even address using WhitePages.com.

••••••••••••••••••••••••

21 http://www.bbb.org/

22 http://consumeraffair.com/

This is what you should create an email address purely to respond to your online dates; it should be completely separate from the one you use on a daily basis. Never use your real name or anything that could identify you when creating this particular address.

And, as I'm sure you all know, if you do happen to miss the signs that the guy you're into is secretly bad to the bone, make sure you meet in a public place during the daylight hours.

It's better to be safe than sorry.

ALICIA'S STORY: I'M LUCKY TO BE ALIVE

"I met a guy through Match who told me his name was Chris. He contacted me but didn't have a picture. I went with it, but this was right when I started online dating and I didn't know better. I said let's meet, fine, fantastic, so we met for drinks at a bar and started seeing one another pretty regularly. He always came to my house, or my neighborhood. It was very casual. But as our relationship progressed, things got weird.

"I never really wondered about where he lived, because my place was more convenient. I was living in downtown Baltimore, while he was south of the city. But eventually I wanted to see his place – and he wouldn't let me. He always made excuses. It was getting painted, it wasn't clean. There was always something. I couldn't go to his house.

"I think he was married and that he lied about his name. I mean, we were dating for a long time; almost a year. I never knew exactly who he was. He never even paid with a credit card when we went out; he always had cash in hand. I once had the chance to look in his wallet, to look for his license, look for any kind of evidence that he actually was who he claimed to be, but I didn't take it. I still regret it.

"It began to creep me out. I have a friend whose parents are private detectives, and they ran his plates for me. His number never came up. I began to think he was like the Craigslist killer.

"Every time I'd challenge him, he'd get really, really angry. But I was thinking, 'This guy knows where I live and I don't want to cause problems.

"Yes, I had a phone number for the guy, but anyone can get a cell phone. You can also set up an email account with any name you want. You can be whoever you want to be.

"When I switched jobs, he called my new place of work and pretended to be someone else. It was too much for me, and it had gone on for too long. I was getting scared, so I decided to end it. But before I could, out of the blue he decided to move to Chicago.

"After he left, I checked for rapes and murders in my area, just to make sure. I felt so stupid. I had met this very charming person, and everything was great, but the outcome was so twisted and weird. To this day it makes me so sick that I didn't know who he was.

"I met my future husband through Match, and on our very first date I insisted he show me his license. He understood. It was a crazy, dark time for me, but I learned my lesson: Make sure they are who they say they are."

CHAPTER 17:

WHAT YOU NEED TO KNOW IN ADVANCE IF YOU'RE CREATING AN ONLINE DATING PROFILE

I'm going to offer up some final words of wisdom in regards to creating an online dating profile and no, I won't be chewing your ear off about safety (this time). But I will warn you that your identity, address and even your personal photographs may be at stake by signing on the dotted line without reading a site's privacy policies.

Your personal details may not be so personal for long

When you're providing your stats to a site like OKCupid or Match, you might not realize that they're saving and cataloging your information for future use. OKCupid readily admits that they might be sending your name, address, email address, telephone number, credit card number, your interests and activities, age and hometown to servers all around the world. If that doesn't fly with you, make sure that you join a site whose policies you're comfortable with. When you think about it, yeah, it *is* creepy that your personal details are out there for every Tom, Dick and Harry to see.

The hidden charges

Do you keep a planner? Are you wisely using your Smartphone to keep a diary of important dates? If not, you should be – especially if you're paying for an online dating site.

You think to yourself, "Match is only $39.95 for one month. I'll try it out, no big deal." But that month comes and goes, as does the next month and you begin to slowly realize that each and every single month, $39.95 is being removed from your account. You think, "What the heck is going on?" You check your credit card statements and realize that your money is being handed to Match, a site you eagerly used for a week before you got bored and eventually forgot you had even signed up for. You think, 'I'm outraged! I only wanted to use it for a month!' That's true, but then you continued to re-sign for the most expensive monthly plan because you had forgotten to cancel your membership. Good luck contesting that one.

Many sites cleverly operate on an automatic monthly billing system so that, if you forget to cancel your account, you're SOL (and I will very nicely alter that expression to "sadly out of luck" because I'm a lady). If you intend to sign up for a short period of time, jot down the date before your service automatically renews. You don't want to make a potentially very expensive mistake.

Also beware sites that offer free trials and still ask you for your credit card information. The same situation applies, and you *will* be charged if you don't cancel in time. If you *don't* meet someone and try to fight for your rights, don't bother; you won't win. Match does, quite thoughtfully, guarantee you six months free if you've purchased a six-month plan and still haven't met anyone you'd actually consider dating. If this sounds like a good option to you, know that you will have to agree not to withdraw your profile and must agree to email a certain number of people per week. However, no one is forcing you to go out with any of the people you've sent messages to. Hallelujah for loopholes!

Play safe with your passwords

This is pretty much a no-brainer.

When you're shopping on a secure server site like Amazon.com or Target.com, you're always asked to pick a secure password. Most sites even tell you how strong your password is. You need to apply the same kind of password to your dating profile, lest you get hacked.

You typically want a password that's a combination of lower and upper case letters and numbers. If your name is Michael and you were born on September 18, you shouldn't choose Michael918 as your code, as it's so obvious. You *could* use a less obvious sequence, like your high school jersey number coupled with the name of your favorite old TV show. You *do* want to stay away from any sort of password that could be associated with your personal information. Partyof591, for example, would be a great password for a guy (because no former athlete in his right mind is going to admit *that Party of Five* was his favorite show in a public forum).

Beware of that fated "Perfect Match" – just when you were about to quit online dating forever

You've been paying for a three month-contract on one of the sites, and your time online is nearly up. You cancel your subscription a day early, but still have the ability to write and respond to emails from other users while still paying for the final month of your membership.

Lo and behold, you get an email from a nearly perfect specimen that very day. He's gorgeous, intelligent, educated and living in your zip code. You write back, but will he see your message in time or is your Cinderella story well and truly over? Or do you renew your account in the hopes that George Gosling's email was fate's way of telling you to stay on the site?

Being a hopeful romantic, you renew your subscription. Alas, you never hear from old not-so-Curious George ever again – because the man (as you knew him anyway) didn't exist: he was a perfectly timed ruse to lure you into renewing your subscription.

"Does this really happen?" you're probably wondering. The answer is YES. In 2010, the federal government forced Australian dating site Red Hot Pie to send an apology email to its members for creating over a thousand fake profiles in order to convince them to stay and pay. [23] In 2005, a similar suit was brought against Match and the now defunct Yahoo! Personals [24] for fraud.

If you don't think you'd be so easily duped, I offer you another word of caution: you never know how the wool can be pulled over your

23 *Lohman, Tim.* November 6 2009. <http://www.computerworld.com.au/article/325344/accc_takes_redhotpie_owners_court/.>

24 *Reuters.* 2005. <http://www.usatoday.com/tech/news/2005-11-18-matchmaking-fraud_x.htm>.

eyes. It's shocking how readily smart people will do stupid things when it comes to love.

CHAPTER 18:

THE LIES WE TELL

Fact: everyone fibs. While we don't always intend to tell an untruth, sometimes it just happens anyway. Even the most pious, honest people on the planet have lied about something at one point or another.

Telling a "little white lie" is especially common when it comes to online dating profiles. It's understandable that you would want to put the best version of yourself out there in order to seem more desirable and more in demand, but sadly, this 'perfect' version of you isn't going to help your cause in the long run; perfection doesn't exist.

While interviewing online daters, one complaint kept cropping up like wildfire: "I wish he would have just have been honest," one woman moaned about the man who lied about his age. "Why couldn't she have just been herself? I'll never go out with her again because she lied to me," a man admonished of a date who appeared on their date 40 pounds heavier than her online photos.

Showing yourself as you used to be years ago isn't going to help your case at all. Even if you've changed your hairstyle in the last *week*, you still need to make sure that's reflected in your profile pictures.

Think about this for a second: You've subtracted a good ten pounds from your waistline by posting an old photo, you've said you just love pro football and that you're fluent in French and Italian. The guy in question happens to be a romance language professor, who, at 30, is the same age you were (when you took that picture, that is) and he's slight. He's not expecting the modern-day version of you.

So when you show up for your date, he doesn't recognize you. He looks all around the restaurant, thinking you might have bailed, and looks resigned as he makes his way over to the bar to have a restorative drink. But then his eyes alight on you and it slowly dawns on him that *you have lied about who you are – and he isn't happy about who you turned out to be.* His look of resignation slowly turns into a grimace of horror.

In the end, your date was *not* dazzled by your amazing personality as you had hoped. You thought, 'Once he has a chance to get to know me, he'll realize I'm still the same person I was in the picture'. You thought that by presenting yourself as you were at your peak, it would inspire this good-looking guy to ask you out. Well, at least you were right about one thing.

Meanwhile, your date is resentful that he's been duped, stays silent for twenty minutes while you to try to impress him with your intelligence and wit, and begs off twenty minutes later without even finishing his Diet Coke, saying that he "forgot" there was somewhere he had to be. Yeah, there's somewhere he has to be, alright – and that's far away from you.

There is no benefit in misrepresenting yourself when online dating. You can't convince a guy to magically become attracted to you, so why try? Move on and find someone who appreciates you for who you are, flaws and all. Don't forget that if you're looking for love online, the options are endless! If one site isn't working in your favor, there are literally hundreds of others to choose from.

The reasons why we would lie are obvious, but what, exactly, do we lie about? Let's explore the fibs men tell first.

According to a recent study[25], men have issues when it comes to their height. While many of them don't quite have Napoleon complexes, they do tack on an extra two to three inches when it comes to standing tall (or short). And no, that was *not* a euphemism for something else, thank

••••••••••••••••••••••••
25 *Rudder, Christian.* July 7 2010. <blog.okcupid.com/index.php/the-biggest-lies-in-online-dating/>

you very much. They generally list themselves at an even 6'0, though they may be anywhere from 5'7 – 5'9.

Guys also lie about their age.[26] Some subtract up to ten years off their actual age, as you'll read about later on in JoJo's story. Ladies, make sure that guys have a healthy amount of photos posted on their page. You can look for clues that the photos are recent too, especially by what's going on in the background. Instead of just looking at their faces, clue in to the circa 1988 New Kids on the Block poster hanging on the wall behind them, especially if he told you he was 25. This isn't exactly a fib, mind, because he *was* 25 once…twenty years ago.

Income is the third thing men stretch the truth about. This is the greatest whopper they tell of all: though a guy might earn $12K a year, he'll make himself sound like he's Daddy Warbucks by saying he earns upwards of $80K. Not that his profession has to mean everything, but when a guy says he's a young business associate and you find out he actually works the fryer at White Castle, well, let's just say you're going to be less than pleased when you do learn the truth.

Women aren't entirely innocent, either. Unsurprisingly, the things we mostly tend to exaggerate about are our physical attributes.

••••••••••••••••••••••••

26 *Rudder, Christian.* July 7 2010. <blog.okcupid.com/index.php/the-biggest-lies-in-online-dating/>

Yes, we lie about our weight – and in a big (pardon the pun) way. The same study found that women who weighed, on average, 148 pounds, listed themselves as being *much* skinnier – a waif-like 110 pounds. Women of a normal to heavy weight also referred to themselves as 'slim' when, in fact, they'd actually fall into the 'sturdy' category.

Like men, however, we're just as likely to lie about our age. We're even bigger liars than the guys are when it comes to this particular whopper, though. While they shave 13 years off the grand total, we subtract 16.

Again, I'll ask the question: why lie? Creating a false persona or a stretched version of the truth is just going to annoy your date and hurt your feelings when you see the displeased look on his or her face. The truth isn't always pretty, but it's even uglier to see someone disappointed when they see who you really are. Just saying.

JOJO'S STORY:
I COUNSELLED, AND DIDN'T CRITICIZE,
MY ONLINE DATE WHEN HE LIED

"I've been an active online dater on a variety of sites for the last two years, but haven't been very successful. I haven't found a surplus of attractive, normal men online in New York City. But when I saw Jared's profile on Match, I thought my luck had finally changed.

"I thought, 'Wow, what a good-looking guy.' He was 40, over six feet tall and claimed to have an athletic build. We also happened to be in the same, very specific field of work. I thought to myself, 'How do I not know this guy?'

"We began to email back and forth and then spoke on the phone a few times. He sounded great. Our communication turned to texting and we eventually started trying to make a plan to go out, which is when he started to get strange. He was very specific about where and when he wanted to meet up. When I would make suggestions, he'd praise them and dismiss them equally as quickly.

"So the night of our date came and it turned out that we were expecting a major blizzard. I asked if he'd prefer to reschedule for a time when a major storm *wasn't he*ading our way but he was adamant that we keep our date. He said, 'No, no, I don't want to reschedule. As long as you don't mind me in my casual clothes, let's meet for a drink. Now, for me, casually dressed means a cute dress with tights and snow boots, meaning that I still looked cute, despite being low-key. I thought that, as a 40-something professional, he would follow suit in his idea of a casual outfit.

"On a side note, going to the gym is really important to me. I go straight after work every single night, five days a week. I suggested we meet up at 8:30 or 9 so that I could still get my work out in, but he told me the 'latest he'd be willing to meet me' was 7 p.m. Now, I would much rather spend an evening sweating it out at the gym then going on another failed online date, but I had high hopes for this guy, so I agreed.

"So I decided to be game about the experience and headed to this random Mexican restaurant he had chosen. In his text message he had said he'd be sitting in the corner of the bar. I get to the bar and don't see anyone in the corner who fit his description or photographs. I did see a muscled man with a tight T-shirt and cheesy tattoos, though. Imagine my surprise when mister motorcycle man started talking to me and said, 'Hey, are you JoJo by chance?'

"I was thrown for a loop. This guy didn't look *anything* like the pictures I had seen. But then he goes, 'Are you looking for Jared? I'm his friend, Paul. Jared just went to the bathroom, but he'll be out in a minute.'

"I was beyond annoyed, thinking '*Really*? He brought a wingman on a first date? What a jerk'. Surprisingly, Paul and I actually started to get along, but mostly because I was making fun of Jared for needing an in-house support system. The indignity of realizing that my date needed a second opinion was only second to realizing that Jared had completely lied about his physical appearance.

"When he came out of the bathroom, it was clear that his pictures were from 10 or 15 years prior. He definitely didn't look like the 40 year-old he claimed to be, but more like late 40s or even his early 50s. He was wearing a matching sweatshirt and sweatpants combo – not the cool kind, but the kind you get at a discount saver store – with white sneakers, white socks and a baseball cap pulled so low over his face that I could barely see his face.

"When he came over and sat down to introduce himself, I couldn't stay annoyed. I just felt so much sympathy for him that he didn't have the confidence to admit who he really was online. I said, 'You're not the guy you said you were and your photos were clearly taken a long time ago.' He was adamant that he hadn't lied, that he really *was* 40. So I told him to prove it, and show me his ID. When he did, he was shamefaced because he was, in fact, 49. What he said to me was, 'No, but really. I'm 40 on the inside'. He was so earnest that I really couldn't hate him for wasting my time.

"We actually wound up having a good, interesting conversation, but I told him there was no way in heck we'd be going out again. I basically acted as his therapist on that date, coaching him on how lying to people was just going to disappoint them and trying to make him realize that he wasn't doing himself any favors by fudging his age. I even schooled him on his clothes and told him, 'This is Manhattan. People don't wear stuff like that out in public.' At the end of the date, though he kept asking me if I was really sure that I wasn't interested, I said, 'I did enjoy having one drink with you, but that's as far as it's going to go. You should know that you're a really fun person to be around, so don't be afraid to be yourself.'

"On a side note, Jared's friend Paul also happened to be meeting a girl from Match that night at the same bar. I found out that he and Jared go out together, pretend they're strangers and schedule their online dates for the same night at the same place so they check out the other person's girl. Paul's date turned out much more positively than Jared's did, though: his girl ended up being very good-looking and they seemed to hit it off so much that they even left the bar together – whereas Jared, of course, left alone."

PART VI:

LOCATION MATTERS

CHAPTER 19:

FUN FACTS ABOUT

ONLINE DATING AROUND THE WORLD

Is the grass really greener on the other side of the pond? Thirty percent of American couples meet a partner online, but do international residents have better luck? Love is meant to be the universal language, but as you know by now, there's an entirely different system of rules when it comes to the weird world of online dating.

♥ **CANADA**
Believe it or not, Canadians are the most active online daters of any nationality. [27] Yep, 25% of *all* Canadians have reportedly looked for love online. It would appear that the website Plenty of Fish has made an impact with our neighbors to the north as well: in

....
27 *Oliveira, Michael.* December 28 2010. <http://www.theglobeandmail.com/news/technology/canadians-spend-more-time-online-than-any-other-country/article1850700/.>

addition to being the world's 331st busiest website, it comes in at number 33 in Canada – just behind power players like CNN and CBC. [28] Crazy, eh?

♥ **ITALY**

Online dating in Europe is *huge*. In fact, folks from the smallest continent rival the U.S. in regards to its number of online daters: over 38 million people go on matchmaking websites each month. Though you might expect that the biggest market for online love would lie in the U.K., it is, in fact, Italy, the country where amore originated that's most active. Nearly 3.5 million users visit sites like ItalianFriendFinder.com, Italiamia.com and ItalianSingles.com each month. Spain and Germany, incidentally, round out the top three European cities where online dating dominates. [29]

♥ **CHINA**

There are over a billion residents in China, and of that number, 180 million are swinging bachelor boys. Halve that, and you've got the

28 *Oliveira, Michael.* March 25 2010. <http://www.the-globeandmail.com/news/technology/personal-tech/canada-a-hotbed-of-online-dating/article1511473/print/>.

29 *Zima.* November 17 2011. <http://www.skadate.com/blog/ska-date-presents-online-dating-statistics-and-interesting-facts.html>.

number of Chinese men who take advantage of online dating sites. Fifty million women also subscribe, making China the most rapidly growing market of online daters in the world. Even if you're not a numbers person, this information should mean something significant for Chinese women: there are literally two men for every woman online in your country right now, which are some damn good odds for meeting the man of your dreams. Get online *now*. And when I say *now*, I mean, like yesterday.

Given that this is a nation that dismisses singletons over the age of 30 by calling them 'shengnan' or 'shengny' (which literally translates to 'left-over man' or 'left-over' woman'), online dating may be one of the best ways to look for love. The most popular dating site is Jiayuan.com. Although there is much to be gained by looking for love online in China, unfortunately you won't be able to do so if you're a soldier: the government legally banned its army from using dating sites in 2010. [30]

• •
30 *Spegele, Brian.* July 2 2010. <http://blogs.wsj.com/chinarealtime/2010/07/02/chinas-troops-lose-a-love-connection/>.

♥ **AFGHANISTAN**

The next time you grumble about the people you're meeting on Match, take a moment of silence for the people of Afghanistan, who are forbidden from using online dating sites. However, this isn't too much of surprise in light of the fact that most marriages are still arranged in the landlocked Asian country.

♥ **IRAN**

As in Afghanistan, online dating is forbidden in Iran. But here's the rub: *all* dating is forbidden in this Islamic nation. Teenage boys and girls are separated until they're of a marrying age, upon which they can be introduced – as long as a family member is doing the setting up. Ouch. I hope their mothers know their types.

♥ **JAPAN**

There are 60 million online daters in Japan, so it *is* deemed socially acceptable despite being a culture where parents still set their kids up with matchmakers (a Japanese custom called Omiai). The government is even behind its residents looking for love online and, to prove it, launched their own website, the Fukui Marriage-Hunting Café.

♥ **UNITED KINGDOM**

Online dating is on the rise for the tea and lager-loving Brits. In fact, 20% of 19-25 year-olds met their future spouses on the 'net (which, when you think about it, is much more refined than meeting a man in a pub). Despite the young marriage demographic, U.K residents aged 55 and up were the most active online daters.

♥ **AUSTRALIA**

There are 1.5 million online daters in Australia, and that number is expected to reach two million by 2020. [31] The country famous for spawning a man who hunted crocodiles for a living also has launched a rather "interesting" dating site: one that's specifically for farmers. Yup, FarmDating.com does exist. So put that in your pipe and grow it.

KATHY'S STORY: AN INTERNATIONAL LOVE MATCH

"I'm originally from Australia and had gotten bored with Australian men. I was working at a women's magazine as a journalist, and my

••••••••••••••••••••••

31 *The Times of India.* July 12, 2010. <http://articles.timesofindia.indiatimes.com/2010-01-12/man-woman/28123708_1_niche-sites-industry-religion>.

editor told me to do a story on online dating. So I joined partially because I was interested in seeing what happened, and partially because I had an assignment.

"I put my details on a bunch of different websites and wanted to see what kind of responses I'd get. I received about 500 emails from men all around the world, but ended up going on about twelve dates in Australia. Some were super creepy and scary, but I wasn't too bothered about long-term potential because I wasn't really seeking anything serious.

"Then I got this email from Tom, who found me on a site called American Singles. We started corresponding non-stop. Our online conversations snowballed to the extent where we were writing unusually long emails to one another every night. After a month of written conversations, we started talking on the phone. Our telephone conversations were epically long, but we lucked out because the phone companies had a deal on at that time.

"One of our phone calls went on for eleven straight hours. It was like going on an all-day date. We'd put the phone down to go and get something to drink or take a bathroom break and come right back to pick up the conversation where we had left off. We got to know each other so well, though all we had was talking and emailing. This was in the era before webcams or Skype, so we had to had to get to know one another the organic way.

"A few months later we decided that we should probably meet face to face, so I flew to New York City to visit him. When he met me at the airport, it was as if I was seeing my long-distance boyfriend, when, in fact, we had never really seen one another aside from a few photographs.

"The scenario seems like it would have been strange, but it was completely comfortable. Tom isn't really my physical type, if I was going to write down what my perfect type was. But at a certain point, after all of our conversations, it didn't really matter what he looked like. I met someone who made me change my idea of what I was looking for. We've now been married for 16 years.

"Based on my experience, my advice is this: don't have preconceived ideas about what you're looking for, and don't be afraid to take a chance. If you're looking at a photo online and thinking, 'He doesn't look like the kind of guy I'd be attracted to', go on a date anyway. What do you have to lose? You never know. It's not just about looks, it's about personality, who they are inside and if they can make you laugh. Don't be so judgmental.

"I'm not saying settle for less, but to go into with less expectations. You're not going to meet Brad Pitt on Match.com, and you shouldn't go into it thinking you will. You never know what might happen, and I'm living proof of that. I was just doing [online dating] out of curiosity. I didn't want to get married and I was against the idea of looking for love online. Much to my surprise, I got swept off my feet."

CHAPTER 20:

THE BEST AMERICAN CITIES TO MEET YOUR ONLINE MATE

Think back to the time (even if it was about five minutes ago) when you created your first online dating profile. One of the first questions you were asked to answer is how far you'd be willing to travel for love. The options are finite. Most sites assume correctly that we want someone who lives in our immediate vicinity (give or take 60 miles), thus making a pending online relationship practical and easy.

Unfortunately, there aren't always a plethora of great options in your city, so some *will* have better luck dating online than others.

Now here's where it gets tricky. Two surveys were done over the past two years, both of which attempted to determine the best American cities to find a mate online. OKCupid obtained their results in 2010 by discovering which cities had the highest number of active user profiles. In 2011, SNAP Interactive, the company responsible for the social dating app Are You Interested, did their own research, compiling data from AreYouInterested.com and the app's Facebook fan page.

So what did they conclude?

OKCUPID'S BEST CITIES TO FIND LOVE

1) **Boston, Massachusetts**
   Percentage of population age 15 and older that is single: 50%

2) **Washington, D.C.**
   Percentage of population age 15 and older that is single: 49%

3) **San Francisco, California**
   Percentage of population age 15 and older that is single: 50%

4) **Seattle, Washington**
   Percentage of population age 15 and older that is single: 47%

5) **Atlanta, Georgia**
   Percentage of population age 15 and older that is single: 48%

6) **Portland, Oregon**
   Percentage of population age 15 and older that is single: 48%

7) **Philadelphia, Pennsylvania**
Percentage of population age 15 and older that is single: 51%

8) **Los Angeles, California**
Percentage of population age 15 and older that is single: 51%

9) **Dallas, Texas**
Percentage of population age 15 and older that is single: 46%

10) **Detroit, Michigan**
Percentage of population age 15 and older that is single: 51%

SNAP INTERACTIVE'S GET LUCKY IN LOVE CITIES

1) New York, New York

2) Houston, Texas

3) Chicago, Illinois

4) Los Angeles, California

5) Denver, Colorado

6) Indianapolis, Indiana

7) Phoenix, Arizona

8) Dallas, Texas

9) Philadelphia, Pennsylvania

But which list is correct? Well, they both are, to a degree. SNAP is correct in saying that the hustle, bustle and ambition of folks living in the Big Apple sometimes makes it impossible to find the necessary time needed to find that perfect match (or even a not so perfect one). Looking for love online is the natural next step for these successful city dwellers.

Similarly, Boston's heavy student presence is the most likely reason it appeared in OKCupid's top spot. More than 50 colleges call Beantown home. Among them: Boston College, Boston University, Harvard, Simmons College, Emerson College, MIT and Northeastern University.

Why did Washington D.C. find itself in the runner-up position on OKCupid's hit list? According to the site's cofounder and CEO, it's because the federal government is the city's biggest employer, which creates a lot of temporary posts and a revolving door of employees looking for love.

"Each new administration brings in a new batch of transplants looking to unwind and commiserate," notes Sam Yagan, who adds that San Francisco made the cut because of its young, tech-savvy population. [32]

••••••••••••••••••••••••
32 *Levy, Francesca.* August 27 2010. <http://www.forbes.com/2010/08/27/online-dating-internet-lifestyle-cities-singles.html>.

The most obvious reason that any of these cities are included is simply because of the high amount of unmarried singles living in each area. Cities can be large and lonely, your life can feel consumed by your job or you can simply be trying to meet people outside of your immediate social circle. Whatever the reason, for many urbanites, it's much easier to socialize with the opposite sex online.

Drexel PhD students Rachel Magee and Christopher Mascaro have also concluded that geographic location is important when it comes to the success of online love stories. In their thesis study, [33] they found that those living in the South Atlantic were the most successful as a region, while California was the luckiest state of love. Houston, Chicago and New York were the top cities for both quality and quantity.

But don't go moving just yet. Just because your city, state or region may not be included in these lists doesn't mean that you can't find love online wherever it is that you happen to be. Love can, and does, happen everywhere.

• •

33 *Faulstick, Britt.* January 5 2012. <>http://www.drexel.edu/now/news-media/releases/archive/2012/January/iSchool-online-dating-study/>.

ABBY'S STORY:
NEW YORK & ENGAGED

"I felt like I had met everyone I was going to meet through my friends and I wasn't meeting any new people, which is crazy because I'm a publicist living in Manhattan. I didn't want to meet people out at a bar, because who ever meets good guys at a bar? You're out and you're drunk. I was 30 and ready to find somebody. I guess I never really thought about settling down until I turned 30 and then a light switched on and I thought, 'Oh my God. I'm 30. I'm ready.'

"I had used up all my available resources, so I decided to try online dating. I certainly didn't think I was going to meet someone. I thought I'd do online dating as a way of killing time and meeting new people.

"In that sense, I got really lucky. Cormaic was the first person I ever went out with that I met on an online dating site, and I was his. We met on OKCupid. It has this star system, where you rate the attractiveness of another user. Everyone knows that you're not really reading the profiles, you're just looking to see how cute the other person is. So we both gave each other really high ratings, messaged back and forth for a while and then met up for a drink on April 1 of 2010. Two months later we were a couple.

"I realized that I was in love with him four

or five months into our relationship. How he felt about us was always clearer to him, but I took it slowly. We would go out once a week, and about two months later we were dating but not official – until he invited me camping with his family over Memorial Day weekend.

"I liked him at that point, and thought, 'If I go three days in the woods with him we'll either be fully together or I'm never going to want to see him again.' We ended up having a really amazing time though; it was a great weekend. After that, we were officially together.

"I realized that I was actually more suited to meeting a man online than meeting someone at a bar or through friends, because people have always told me I'm not the warmest person in the world; it takes me awhile to open up. Online you can look at someone's profile and it's a little less threatening to message someone back and forth and get to know them as opposed to meeting them right away without getting a sense of who they are.

"In fact, we just got engaged, and though it's weird, I'm still a little leery of telling people that we met online. It seems so impersonal. That said, my point of view is that it's just luck anytime you meet somebody, so it doesn't matter where you meet them. You might as well give online dating a shot and see where it goes.

LACEY'S STORY:
LOS ANGELES & MARRIED

"I met my husband, Justin, on eHarmony. I had been on the site for two months when he emailed me. It was a slow process. He'd submit questions, I'd answer. Then I'd submit similar questions to him. He sent me three things he liked, I sent him three things I liked. From there we progressed to short answer questions and eventually, emails. This is just the way that eHarmony works. It's a lengthy process – our first stage took about a month – but it's worth it.

"We continued to email one another for another month before we finally set up our first date. By then I thought I knew him pretty well, or at least knew enough about him to know we'd get along. I really appreciated that he didn't push me to go out right away and let me get to know him online first.

"We went to a Mexican restaurant in Santa Monica for our first date, which lasted for three hours. It was two hours before we even ordered dinner. The waiter had to come over three times before we even picked up our menus, we were that immersed in the conversation.

"He didn't hide anything or hold anything back. We discovered that we were even more alike than we had initially thought and had many of the same interests. We also have the same thoughts about family, love and what we want from our futures.

"After that, we texted and talked on the phone. I was going out of town the following weekend and we hadn't set up another date yet. I was at the airport and a cute guy was hitting on me, so I text Justin and asked *him* if we were going out again; I didn't want to pursue anything with anyone else if we were. He wrote me back that he had been waiting for me to return from my trip before he asked me on a second date, which was a relief. From there we gradually began to see each other once a week, then three times a week, then finally every single night. We're now married.

"Our relationship progressed like a natural relationship would, aside from how we met. I would never have met him if it weren't for eHarmony. We live in different parts of LA and our friends have different interests; we would never have been in the same place at the same time.

"So my advice to any potential online daters would be to stick with it. I did meet nice guys, but we didn't have a lot in common and we weren't in the same place relationship-wise. I didn't meet Justin until my sixth year of online dating! There's a ton of fish in the sea – it's just about finding the right one for you. You can never tell which one is going to bite!"

JULIA'S STORY:
CHICAGO & SINGLE

"I had just gotten out of a nearly four-year relationship with the man I thought I would marry. We were living together, had gone ring shopping and both of our families expected it to happen. He began pulling away bit by bit until it was obvious that it was over. It took me a year to pull myself out of the bleakness that occurred after our breakup.

"When I was finally ready to start dating again, I joined OKCupid. I made a profile on Match, but chickened out before I actually put it up. Everyone just seemed so scary and corporate, which isn't my scene at all. I felt like I was going to a happy hour in the Loop instead of Logan's Square.

"OKCupid is much better in Chicago. The guys are trendy, artsy, cute and funny. You'll find more beards and flannel than CEOS in suits. They might be CEOs underneath, but that won't be the first thing you notice about them.

"Since joining the site, I've been out with five people. The guys that worked out live in my neighborhood and had a lot in common with me. In fact, one guy had a 99% Match rating – which is about the highest you can get. None of them has been quite right yet, but they're all cute, interesting and fun. Seriously, there are a lot of cute potential boyfriends in Chicago. I have to pace myself, of course, so I'll respond to maybe 2% of the people that contact me. I'm selective because I can be; there's a lot out there.

"I've realized that I prefer online dating because I have a lot of deal breakers, which tends to be what happens when you get older and have been through enough bad situations. I like seeing that people share the same core stuff that's important to me.

"I know that I'm not ready for a relationship right now. I'm just seeing what's out there and figuring out what I want. I'm not ready to settle down with a guy who isn't exactly what I'm looking for. The dates I'm going on aren't diversions – I'm giving them a chance and hoping that they'll work out – but if, after however many dates, I realize that they're not right in the long run, I'm not going to keep up pretenses.

"Unfortunately, the downside is that although I'm just having fun and seeing what's out there, the people I've met are looking for something serious. There are so many expectations involved when you're online dating, and so many hopes that I'm going to be the perfect person for them. Knowing that I might have to end something in the near future is uncomfortable, but I'm not going to settle, either."

CHAPTER 21:

ONLINE LOVE
SUCCESS STORIES

By this point, you've heard mostly about the downside of the online dating industry. But remember this: 17% of all Americans meet their spouse online these days, and I wouldn't be surprised if that percentage rapidly increased in the next coming years. You *can* meet the love of your life (or at least someone you call husband/wife) online – and these fine folks are the living proof.

JAKE'S STORY:
WHY TAKING ADVANTAGE OF
A FREE TRIAL WEEKEND WAS
THE BEST DECISION OF MY LIFE

"In the late spring/early summer of 2007, Match.com was offering a free trial weekend. You would sign up as normal, but you could try out the site for free before they actually charged you. If you didn't like it, you could cancel – no strings attached. Because of the time constraints, I set up my account very quickly. I put up a single line of information that read as follows (which I remember verbatim because my now-wife still quotes it to this day): 'I find far too many things far too funny.' "I didn't even put up a picture.

"The next morning I received a message from Linda, the woman who would eventually became my wife. We exchanged a few messages that day. On the second day, we exchanged contact info and talked on the phone for the remainder of the free weekend. Because I was already chatting with her, I cancelled my account before the weekend was up.

"The following weekend we met up for dinner. I took her to a restaurant in Providence, RI, and we clearly had a great time. From that point on, we were dating. Three weeks after we started dating, she had plans to attend a week-long music festival in upstate New York. She invited me, so I took a week off of work and went with her.

"After we returned from that week away together, we headed to her apartment. I had a week's worth of clothes and most of the belongings I needed to get by for a while, and I just never left. I moved in. Less than four weeks after our first date, I had a copy of her apartment key and was chipping in on her portion of the rent (she was living with two other roommates at the time). Less than a year later, I proposed and a year after that, we were married. Just after that we bought a house, and now we have a baby boy. Taking advantage of that free weekend was the smartest thing I've ever done."

HAYLIE'S STORY:
I FOUND THE MAN WHO
MAKES ME A BETTER PERSON

"I met Tyler on Match.com in October of 2011. Mind you, I had winked at and emailed him earlier in the summer, but he later told me that he had been dating another girl from Match at the time – which didn't work out. So, he finally contacted me and we talked on the phone, emailed and texted for a good week before actually meeting in person. Because I had been on a recent string of bad dates and he lived about an hour away, I was a little gun shy about going out with someone else from Match, but I sucked it up and went anyway.

"We had a great conversation over dinner, but I can be a little shy sometimes so thought the date might not be going well. We went our separate ways after the meal and I thought to myself, 'Well, that's it. Another failure of a date'.

"But I did end up hearing from Tyler again, and the funny thing was, he didn't think our date had gone badly at all. In fact, he was surprised at

211

how simple and easy it was, and even mentioned that there was a lack of those awkward moments you so often have on first online dates.

"Our second date came soon after and we decided to try something a little outside the box by going on a 12-mile bike ride. It was literally one of the best dates I've ever had. We both like the outdoors, we were comfortable with each other and we joked and laughed the entire time.

"From that day on, we quickly became a couple. He's taught me so many things, from how to make apple cider to how to build a deck. I feel not only as if I'm always learning something new when I'm around him, but also how to be a better person in general.

"I don't think he knows just how much he's taught me, or how much it means to me that he's motivated me. He's a very active person and he's been a great help to get my butt in gear and set goals for myself. I'm not sure I would have had the strength or the confidence to accomplish what I've done in the past year without him. He has also taught me to never give up on my dreams, because I know now that one day, with his help, I'll reach them. Meeting Tyler was worth every bad date and every stupid email I ever received. I guess you could safely say that I'm glad I joined an online dating site."

KIM'S STORY:
I WENT THE DISTANCE FOR LOVE

"At the age of 30, I decided that I wasn't having much luck (and didn't enjoy) meeting people out at bars. All of my friends were doing the online dating thing, but I wasn't sure. I thought I'd be embarrassed to do it, but I wasn't getting any younger and I was getting down on myself that I hadn't met someone, so I finally caved and joined eHarmony.

"My now-fiancé and I lived about two hours away from one another at the time – I was living in Rhode Island and he was living in Connecticut – so I suggested that we meet halfway for our first date. Aside from that, my only other request was that we meet during the daytime. I always thought nighttime dates could lead to physical stuff, and I didn't want to go there. Otherwise, I told him he could call the shots and plan the date.

"We wound up meeting for lunch in Mystic, Conn. I had gotten there first (because, as I was soon to find out, he always runs about 15 minutes behind schedule) and I was hiding behind a bush in front of the restaurant. He had texted me that he was coming down the street, so I emerged from my hiding place. He still tells me that the second I walked out from behind that bush he instantly fell in love with me – and the feeling was mutual. We definitely had an instant connection.

"He looked exactly like his picture, though I found him even more attractive in person. So we went to lunch, and then for a drink and then coffee after that. We had five and a half hours worth of nonstop conversation. Not for one second did we have that awkwardness of not having something to talk about. After the date I thought to myself, 'I could marry this guy.' I still have a text message he sent me eight days after our first date, saying, 'Will you marry my crazy self one day?' We knew a week into the relationship.

"eHarmony was so accurate about matching us together. It gave him a good idea of who I was and vice versa. We're compatible on almost every level. We have common interests and balance each other out perfectly. The only inaccuracy was our distance. We fell outside the distance parameters, as we both put in that we would date someone up to 60 miles away and at the time, he was living 74 miles away from me. It was a lucky mistake though. I ultimately ended up moving to be with him three months into our relationship.

"We got engaged three months after we moved in together. Everything happened very quickly. He was going to be 35 and I had just turned 31. We knew we were meant for each other, so we thought, 'Why are we going to continue waiting?' Because we're a little older, we knew what we wanted right away, and that was to get married and start a family. And to think that I was only on eHarmony for one month...and that he was the second guy I went out with from the site. That was the last first date I'll ever have.

"I'm glad I got over my embarrassment enough to try online dating. We all know that that's how most people are meeting their partners nowadays, so why not have a little faith? There is someone out there for everyone and online dating really does work. Just be patient, because you never know who you're going to meet and how you're going to meet him."

CHAPTER 22:

SUMMING IT UP

There's a ton of information for you to process here, I know. Hopefully you've picked up some practical tips and can successfully – and safely – navigate through the online dating world.

But let's do a quick refresher, just in case your brain is in overload mode.

You've learned:

♥ What site is right for you

♥ That you might just be pickier than you thought

♥ How to get out of a bad date

♥ How to dress and where to go on your first online date

♥ The safety precautions you need to take

♥ How to style yourself for your online dating profile photo

- ♥ That you should never, under any circumstance, lie about who you are

- ♥ How to spot players and cheaters

- ♥ How to create a great profile

CHALLENGE: Be open. Don't say "no" to that person just because they don't look like your 'type.' Though good photos can be deceiving, the opposite is true as well; some people just aren't photogenic. If you're really looking for love, what do you have to lose?

SECTION 2:

FACEBOOK

If you exist in the 21st century and don't live under a rock, you use Facebook. The site is so mainstream that it's actually managed to integrate itself into pretty much one out of every five conversations you'll hear on the street. "So I was checking out his Facebook page and…" you'll hear. Or, "Why hasn't she accepted my friend request yet? Why is she playing that game?" you might hear one guy say to another as he bikes down your street.

Heck, Facebook is such a socially accepted thing these days that most guys you meet out even ask for your account information before they ask for your number! That's some ass backwards behavior if you ask me. But never mind that – an Oscar-nominated movie was even made about the site's creation…and it starred Justin Timberlake.

So now let's look at some numbers to back up the facts. In 2011, more than 800 million people worldwide were actively using the site. More than 50% of those people (including myself) log on to the site every single day. Given these statistics, it's safe to say that much of what you say and do is going to be seen by anyone you haven't remembered to use a privacy setting on. This probably includes at least one potential suitor and a few ex-partners.

Given the sheer amount of people you're going to be friend accepting on a daily basis, you've got to be extra careful about how you present yourself, what pictures you personally post and which friends you allow to tag *you* in photos. Much more than your love life could be hurt by what goes on your wall. Potential employers might see a photo of you doing a keg stand, or your parents might find out about that night that you played strip poker with seven guys and lost. Be aware that *you* may lose many things – and people – in your life depending upon how you choose to portray yourself on Facebook.

PART I:

FACEBOOK – A GREAT WAY TO DATE

CHAPTER 23:

FACEBOOK, THE 'LEGIT' NON-DATING/DATING SITE

In 2010's *The Social Network*, Mark Zuckerberg (played by Jesse Eisenberg) comes up with the idea behind Facebook after his girlfriend dumps him. Out of spite, he creates an on-campus only website called Facemash which rates the attractiveness of Harvard University's co-eds. The site morphed into something called TheFaceBook, which then became the monster it is today. When it went public in 2012, Facebook was worth $104 billion and had 955 million users.[34]

So you could say, in conclusion, that sometimes, breaking up can be a good thing. But is the site good for hooking up as well? The answer here is yes, yes, YES (that was supposed to convey a *When Harry Met Sally* style orgasm, FYI).

Though Zuckerberg was inspired to create the site out of spite for an ex, Facebook is actually one of the best places on the net to make a love match.

34 *Wikipedia*. October 1, 2012. <http://en.wikipedia.org/wiki/Facebook>.

While people using online dating sites have the potential to gravely misrepresent themselves, what you see on Facebook is what you get.

Most people will be open about what they do for work and aren't shy about revealing who they are through photographs. Zuckerberg realized one very sage truth about humanity in creating the site, and that is that we're all closet narcissists with voyeuristic tendencies. Therein lies the beauty of Facebook. For the most part, we are all too proud of displaying who we are to lie about ourselves. Plus, most of us don't specifically use the 'Book as a dating site, so we aren't as worried about how we look to a potential love interest.

Although 1 in 5 singles meet their partner online these days, a Stanford University/City College of New York study[35] states that meeting through friends is still the most common practice of all. Facebook, then, is an excellent way to blend modern and standard dating practices, as you're technically meeting through friends...who also happen to be online.

Facebook is actually the most honest "dating" site out there. You can grill your friends for information on their friends and really make certain and get key pieces of information you wouldn't ordinarily be able to obtain from a stranger you

35 *Rosenfeld, Michael J.* <www.stanford.edu/%7Emrosenfe/ Rosenfeld_How_Couples_Meet_Working_Paper.pdf>.

met on the street or a match you made on an on-line matchmaking site. You can also poke, friend request and message someone you don't know if you're feeling particularly brazen. You don't know them; there' no reason to feel embarrassed or shy.

Facebook can be a great dating tool if you're using it in the right way. Here's what you need to know:

1) **Have a "normal" profile picture**
   Because most people keep their profiles hidden, your one shot at intriguing someone of the opposite sex is your profile picture, which anyone can see (unless you request to be rendered unsearchable, that is.) Therefore, you want to make sure that you look approachable and non-threatening, so use a photo of yourself shot from the waist up. Using a far away photo of yourself won't even hint at what your face looks like, while a close-up won't indicate what your body shape might be. Show just enough of yourself that you're giving others a clear picture of what you look like. Above all else, make sure you're smiling in the photo; nobody wants to befriend a misery guts.

2) **Change Privacy Settings to "Friends of Friends"**
   You have three general options when it comes to who can see what on Facebook.

There's "Friends Only," "Friends of Friends" and "Everyone." Most people choose the "Friends Only" option if they're overly cautious about who's seeing what. But if you're looking to expand your network to include potential partners, you want to change your settings to "Friends of Friends." I'd avoid opting for "Everyone" though – you never know what drama you're opening yourself up to if your profile is accessible to the world.

3) **Don't post anything too personal about yourself**

   If you're allowing complete strangers to see your profile, you want to limit how much you're revealing. You never know who's checking you out – be it a potential employer or future boyfriend – so you don't want to be announcing to the world at large that you got 'so hammered and made bad decisions' last night, right?

4) **Have an interesting 'About' section**

   Facebook is not an online dating site, so don't treat it as such. You never want to say that you enjoy long, romantic walks on the beach. Instead, be as open as possible about who you are and what your interests are.

Remember, everyone is unique – so don't be afraid to show what makes you different.

5) **Be proactive**
If you see someone you like, why not message him or her? As long as you don't sound like a creepy stalker, you have absolutely nothing to lose! Keep it simple and say, "Hi! I'm a friend of Allison's too, and I thought you looked interesting/like someone I wanted to know." Then finish up by asking a question akin to "How do you like living in so and so" or "How's your day?" When you finish with a question, you're giving the person you've written to an opening to respond.

Now that you have some concrete guidelines, what are you waiting for? Go find someone you're attracted to and boldly send that persona message. I triple doggy dare you… And yes, that *is* a direct challenge.

DEREK'S STORY: THE REASON I LOOK FOR GIRLS ON FACEBOOK IS…

"I have never, ever been into online dating. It's not my thing. I always find that the girls that use those sites are either desperate or ready for marriage. I am neither of those things, and I prefer to meet women the organic way: via Facebook.

"I mean, I do meet women while I'm out and about, but I work in finance, and I don't have a lot of free time on my hands. I'm at my desk for more than 12 hours a day most days. I'm not going to sit behind it for another four hours scouting for girls I have to put a ton of effort into by using an online dating site.

"I'd rather know what I'm getting up front, so I search through the friends of my female friends until I find someone I'm attracted to that lives in the area. I'll always poke the girl right away and I'll usually send her a message too if she's really attractive. I don't usually tell my female friends I'm doing this, because women like to talk, and I don't want the girl to know how I found her.

"I like knowing that she's someone who's in my extended network, that I could easily get the scoop on her should I need to. After one date it's pretty easy to tell whether or not I vibe with someone, so I don't really need all the particulars when I'm not invested. If, after a few dates, I think I'm beginning to fall, I might then find out what her deal is. Then again, I might not.

"Plus, I have some really hot female friends. It's just a given that where there's one beautiful girl, many more will follow. At least on Facebook you have the option of knowing she is who she says she is and looks how she claims to look. How can you know that a woman you've never met on a dating website didn't take her picture ages ago and hasn't gained fifty pounds? You can't – and then you're stuck out with someone you'd never in a million years be interested in. No thank you."

LINDSAY'S STORY: I FOUND LOVE THROUGH FACEBOOK

"Stephen and I both went to the University of Maryland, but he was a year older. We had several friends in common, especially in his fraternity, ZBT. We had crossed paths throughout college but were always just acquaintances.

"I actually went to several formals and parties with a few of his fraternity brothers (and may have even dated one or two, if I'm being honest), and he was friendly with a lot of my sorority sisters (still being honest, he may have made out with one or two). We were both in the business school, so it's possible we were even in some of the same classes, though we didn't realize it at the time. But other than a hello here and there, we didn't have any relationship to speak of other than knowing *of* one another.

"After college, I kept up a friendship with one of our mutual friends, Todd. Over the years post-college, I would periodically ask Todd to set me up with his friends – law school classmates, work friends, etc. At one point I remember him asking "What about Stephen?" Because I lived in New York and Stephen still lived in Maryland, I dismissed the idea.

"Fast forward to October 2011, seven years after my college graduation and eight after Stephen's. I've been through my share of relationships — good and bad, long and short — as had he. Living in NYC, I found it impossible to ever meet anyone with completely sincere intentions that I could picture myself with forever.

"I had pretty much given up on the thought that I would be ever get married and got to a place where I was happy with my life as a perpetually single girl. I was supporting myself, had great friends and a good job in one of the most amazing cities on the planet.

"One day I logged on to Facebook at work. Stephen had randomly messaged me out of the blue to say hi. He was in the same place as I was that moment – ready for the day to be over and wanting to kill a little time chatting with whoever was signed on. We had our mutual friend, Todd, to talk about, as he was about to get married.

"But then the next day, we Facebook chatted again. He actually had a few dates lined up for the weekend, so I was giving him helpful pointers, making fun of him and *maybe* flirting just a little bit. The following Monday we were back at it. I asked him how the dates went and we proceeded to talk a little bit more…on Facebook.

"By Wednesday, we had moved on to G-chat, which made it much easier to talk and get work done simultaneously. Not more than a day or two later (after excessive amounts of G-chatting and Facebook chatting, Stephen went out on a HUGE limb and asked me to come to a wedding with him. I went, of course. After the wedding, we started dating and have been in a long distance relationship ever since.

"I think Facebook played a huge role in getting us together. Even with friends saying we would be a good match, I dismissed the idea because of the distance. The realistic way to meet someone – or so I thought – was finding a guy in New York that could fit into my life here and who had common interests and a similar lifestyle. I was wrong. Stephen and I have more in common than anyone I've ever met.

"Meeting at a time when we were both ready for a commitment in addition to starting it over Facebook, where we had a chance to really get to know one another before we started dating, was the perfect way to start our relationship. Without Facebook, we wouldn't be together."

PART II:

THE FACEBOOK RULES

CHAPTER 24:

FACEBOOK DOs & DON'Ts

LESSON #1 ERASE "IT'S COMPLICATED" FROM YOUR VOCABULARY

As far as Facebook relationship statues go, "It's complicated" is the devil. I apologize in advance to the pre-teens reading this, but that particular status is like, *so* junior high.

It's a fact of life that men hate to be pressured into doing anything. The second they feel like you're trying to pin them down, they bolt. This is, effectively, what any woman is doing by posting "It's complicated" as her relationship status. Not only are you *being* overly dramatic, but you're also effectively preventing other members of the opposite sex from pursuing you because they don't want to be tangled up in what appears to be a messy, dramatic situation.

Yeah, your love life very well might be complicated, but why in God's good name does the entire world (or at the very least, all of your acquaintances) need to know about it?

LESSON #2 FOR THE LOVE OF GOD, DON'T POST LOVE POEMS

I'm going to give you some tough love right now. If you have ever posted "Dance like nobody's watching; Love like you've never been hurt. Sing like nobody's listening. Live like it's heaven on Earth" (you know who you are) then you need to check your cheese factor. This is serious, grade-A, high-quality Velveeta.

I know, I know...it seemed deep at the time. But take a second and assess how you would feel if a person you potentially liked had that quote written on his or her wall? Exactly. It isn't sensitive or prolific, it's corny – and corny doesn't belong on your Facebook page. Save it for when you're journaling at night.

LESSON #3 TO AVOID TROUBLE, CONTROL WHO SEES WHAT

Privacy settings exist for a reason: there are certain people who really don't need to see certain (most) things. The more inventive founder Zuckerberg and Co. become, the more problems you're going to have.

That clever social networker has developed software for his site that allows your friends to check you in to certain places. This could be pretty damn bad for a relationship if you lied to your respective other and cancelled your Friday night date under the guise of working late when, in actuality, just wanted to go clubbing with your friends. If your honey sees that one of your drunk friends thoughtlessly checked you into some Hollywood hot spot or another at 1 AM, needless to say he isn't going to be happy and you're going to be in heaps of trouble.

There *are* ways of controlling who sees what and who's allowed to post, tag and check you into places, but it's *your* job to stay on top of it. When you add a new friend, be aware of just how well you know that person…and how much you want them to see. With all the new privacy settings, you'll have no one to blame but yourself if crap hits the proverbial fan.

LESSON #4 HIDE YOUR FRIEND LISTS

Yes, it sounds super shady, but who cares? Though some might be suspicious if they can't see your friends, let me explain why it's actually a smart, preventative measure.

Let's say, for argument's sake, that your friend list is visible to everyone. Let's also say that you bring the guy you've been seeing as your date to a party. You introduce him to one of your casual female acquaintances and wander off to chat to some friends, leaving them behind together. They hit it off, but you don't realize it. He's attracted to your part-time pal but out of respect to you doesn't ask for her number. She, however, is not as respectful. She sifts through your Facebook friends until she finds him, messages him and BOOM! You two are through.

If you think it's an unlikely scenario, wise up. This happens All. The. Time.

LESSON #5 IF YOU CAN HELP IT, DON'T ADD A POTENTIAL LOVE INTEREST

In the play *Lady Windermere's Fan*, Oscar Wilde writes: "I can resist everything but temptation." In a nutshell, this is the reason why you must avoid accepting or requesting a potential love interest as your Facebook friend.

Although a man will idly look through your photographs when you first become friends, the woman in question will be much more likely to frequently 'cyber stalk' the object of her affection. What was once a small crush morphs into a big-scale obsession as you look at his every picture, every status update and each and every comment from another female. Your green-eyed monster comes out to play. You get increasingly depressed as you realize that he has quite a lot of time to play on Facebook, but he has not yet had the time to ask you out.

You decide that you love him, despite barely knowing him. You walk around in a sulk until your friends demand that you snap out of it because your apathy is starting to become depressing. Seriously, your apathy is starting to even depress *me*, and this is a completely fictional situation.

KELLY'S STORY:
I LEARNED MY LESSON THE HARD WAY & NEVER WILL BECOME FACEBOOK FRIENDS WITH A GUY I WANT TO DATE EVER AGAIN

"I didn't expect much when I met Michael. We had met on an online dating site and had been talking for a few weeks before we decided to meet up. I wasn't all that excited to be meeting him in person, though. If I'm being honest, I didn't find him all that attractive. But he was funny and nice, so I finally agreed to meet him for lunch.

"It was a pleasant surprise to discover that Michael was actually *very* attractive in person. We had one of those dream first dates that you always read about in books and see in movies but never seem to happen in real life. We sat, laughed hysterically and talked for four hours. We sparked. I was really happy, because I hadn't felt that way on a first date in years. He had a great, sarcastic sense of humor, he was tall, handsome and had his priorities straight. He was the perfect man.

"In the middle of our date, he got a call from his roommate saying that his dog had thrown up all over the house, and he needed to come home and clean it up. He wanted to keep on hanging out with me, though. I thought that was too random a line to be a lie, so I followed him home.

"He didn't put any moves on me that night at all. We had a blast together though, watching movies and messing around on his computer laughing at ridiculous YouTube videos. During the computer portion of the night, he announced that he was friending me on Facebook.

"I didn't accept immediately, but waited five days after our date. Before I ever accept a potential romantic interest as a friend, I always clean up my page by detagging myself from revealing photos and erasing anything that could be construed as incriminating. I do have a lot of shots where I'm at parties, or wearing very little though. I can't even begin to think what might have been posted on my wall (or by whom) but I thought I had done a good job of getting rid of anything bad.

"I'm not sure what happened, but as soon as I accepted Michael's Facebook friend request, he stopped contacting me completely. I thought I had hidden everything that might have appeared scandalous or negative, but I guess he must have seen *something* that he didn't like, because I never heard from my potential dream man ever again."

CORY'S STORY:
HE TRICKED ME WITH
HIS FACEBOOK PHOTOS!

"I met a guy on Facebook a few years ago who seemed very nice and who also happened to be very attractive; he had a ton of cute photographs, so I knew he was who he claimed to be. I always make it a rule to only pursue or date people who have a lot of photos as opposed to just one or two, so I know that not only are they real, but that they didn't just get lucky with a few really good pictures.

"So after a few weeks of getting to know one another and talking back and forth, we decided to go on a date. We planned to see a movie and then go to dinner afterwards.

"I arrived at the theater before he did and waited nervously. Though we really hit it off online, you never know how a relationship will translate from the virtual world to reality. I was waiting with bated breath when I saw him get out of his car and walk towards me. I was relieved – and really, really happy – to see that he looked exactly like his Facebook photos. But as he got closer, I started to realize that something was missing, but couldn't quite put my finger on what it was…

"…until he greeted me with a big smile and an enthusiastic 'Hi!', whereupon I realized that his four front teeth were missing in action. As I flashed back in horror to all his photos on Facebook, I realized he never once ever posted a photo with an open mouthed smile. I just assumed he was serious and trying to look sexy in his snaps.

"The only thing that took me away from the shock of his missing teeth was the nauseating stench that followed his boisterous "Hi!" Any hope I had previously clung to that his MIA choppers were from some rugged and manly accident like a hockey injury flew right out the window: his not-so-pearly-or-present whites (and not so white, either, come to think of it) were missing from a pure and simple lack of hygiene.

"I decided to suck it up and go to the movie with him. I had, after all, already purchased the tickets. I made it through about 30 minutes of the film before I started noticing that the people around us were starting to make faces and sounds of disgust at the sounds of his heavy panting and smell of his breath. I had to get out of there – and quickly. I figured it would be less humiliating for me to duck out early then try to tough it out and risk tossing my cookies in the theater. I excused myself to the restroom, got in my car and left.

"I later emailed him an apology and was honest with, telling him the exact reason why I had left. He thanked me, telling me that no one ever told him the truth about his horrific smell. At least he knew why his dates seemed to run away! In the end, we both gained something from the experience. He learned that he had a hygiene problem, while I learned to always look for photos with an open mouth smile. Live and learn!"

PART III:

HOW TO BE PHOTO-FRIENDLY

CHAPTER 25:

A FACEBOOK PHOTO TUTORIAL

Be careful…you *ARE* being judged.

Famed photographer Richard Avedon once said: "All photographs are accurate. None of them is the truth." He's right. Photos can't lie: every captured memory is something we have done, for better or worse. However, they may not always tell the complete truth…or, for that matter, the truth as it exists today.

What do I mean? Say you're constantly being snapped at parties with a drink in your hand. An average person looking at your albums would think, "God, that girl is such a lush!" Perhaps they wouldn't take you seriously.

But here's the thing: you're a girl who hates having her photo taken. You're only around snap-happy people at parties, which, on average, is once a month. You're also a teetotaler; the drinks in your hand are always club soda with lime.

So you see what I mean. People draw their own conclusions without having all the facts, which is just one of the reasons why public photographs on Facebook are dangerous.

Let's use Halloween as another example. As Lindsay Lohan's *Mean Girls* character, Cady Harron, says: "In the regular world, Halloween is when children dress up in costumes and beg for candy. In Girl World, Halloween is the one night a year when a girl can dress like a total slut and no other girls can say anything about it. The hard-core girls just wear lingerie and some form of animal's ears."

I agree with her (or, more specifically, agree with Tina Fey, who wrote the script). But if a guy you're dating happens to see photographs of you dressed up as Jessica Rabbit or playing kinky nurse, he's going to get ideas about who you are that aren't accurate or positive. And if Halloween is the one time a year you dress like a hoe, that power to you – many girls do it every weekend!

In a sense, your Facebook profile does define who you are. It says, "This is the image I want to project to the world. I like me in this photograph."

There are several different types of Facebook profile photos. There are the action shots – people who want to portray their daredevil side by showing themselves skydiving, bungee jumping or white water rafting – and those who want to show just how cultured they are by posing in front of iconic monuments like the Leaning Tower of Pisa or the Louvre.

Then, there are those who constantly use the "I'm hot stuff" model pose: cheeks sucked in, arms akimbo, head tilted, makeup applied to perfection.

Given how many people use Facebook and how socially accepted it is, it's very important to be cognizant of what your profile picture might be saying about you. As the main image on your page, the thumbnail that pops up any time you contact someone and the first thing a person sees when they're trying to find out more about you.

Remember, most men like women who appear to be natural and fun, while most women like just about any guy who isn't wearing Hammer Pants. That said, avoid doing the following in your Facebook profile photos at all costs:

1) Don't have a drink in hand; you won't be taken seriously.

2) If you're a girl (or a man with boobs) make sure the ladies are tucked in. Less is more. You don't need to display all you've got to be sexy.

3) Girls, don't pose with friends. Men get confused easily; they don't get why you feel the need to add someone else in to *your* profile picture.

4) Don't change your photo more than once a week. It's annoying and you'll look like you're having an identity crisis.

5) Don't pose with a celebrity. You'll either get a reputation as a groupie or you'll look like you're trying too hard. On the flip side, your single friends will *love* it!

CHAPTER 26:

SHOULD A/YOUR MAN EVER BE INCLUDED IN YOUR PROFILE PICTURE?

I once had a friend who took an adorable photo with a guy she had just started to see. She was so enamored with the shot that she automatically made it her profile picture. I called her immediately with an "abort mission" cry – and made her take that sucker down. She, of course, was confused. Really, what had she done so wrong? It was a cute photo, she protested. She looked good. Unfortunately, my pal was totally missing the point: you *do not make a guy that hasn't yet determined whether or not he wants to be your boyfriend your primary Facebook photo…EVER.*

My pal, who'll we'll call "Sarah" was acting as if she and "Tim" were already exclusive, though he had never once indicated that he wanted to be in a committed relationship. If he had seen the photograph, he would have felt pressure and run in the opposite direction. Men do hate being cornered, after all. As it happened, he felt the overspill of her anxiety about the situation anyway and called off their fling soon after.

Your Facebook profile is about *you*. It's obnoxious for others to see you posing with friends or lovers. And really, why do you feel the need to always pose with someone else? Are you insecure? Do you need to appear as if you have friends? Because we all know you do...we can see your list!

Keep your profile photo as just you, especially if you're trying to use Facebook as a dating tool. You'll be fairly representing yourself on an online community where honesty is *mostly* required.

But back to the boys. Many women include a photograph of themselves posing with a purely platonic male friend. Though Facebook isn't all about dating, to be fair, others might incorrectly assume that you're taken despite having a relationship status that either a) states your single or b) indicates nothing at all.

If that doesn't bother you, great. But personally, as much as I love him, I don't want the world thinking I'm dating my best guy friend. Do you?

PART IV:

FREQUENTLY ASKED FACEBOOK QUESTIONS

CHAPTER 27:

TO POKE OR NOT TO POKE, THAT IS THE QUESTION

If the Facebook "poke" confuses you, you're not alone. I conducted a study based on the opinions of 100 20-40 year-olds, and 97% agreed that the poke was pointless.

But what it is?

According to technology website ROM Cartridge, the poke "is a feature of Facebook whose sole purpose is to attract the attention of another user. The only thing that happens when you poke someone is that this person receives a poke alert on his or her home page. Users can only poke a confirmed friend, someone in a shared network, or a friend of a friend."

Essentially, a poke is a way of introductory flirting. It shows someone that you're interested without going out of your way to put much effort or thought in.

Everyone who exists in cyberspace is hiding behind their computer to some degree, so the poke seems rather spineless. It's for those who don't have the guts to say "I'm interested" straight away. They'd prefer to test the waters and see if they get a reciprocated "poke" back.

Let's put it this way. Do you remember sending your elementary school beloved a note with "Do you like me? Check yes or no"? Poking is the adult equivalent. I'd prefer the note, thanks.

If "To poke or not to poke?" is the question, here's your answer: don't do it unless you're a teenage boy...or you happen to have a big thing for *Beavis & Butthead*.

JACK'S STORY:
SHE DOESN'T WRITE, SHE DOESN'T CALL...
SHE ONLY POKES, AND I HATE IT

"Nina and I met in person when I was on a business trip to San Francisco and decided we liked one another enough to keep in touch. We ended up developing a relationship over Facebook. I wrote a bio all about myself and she did the same. We would send lengthy messages to one another every other day; we really got to know one another well.

"We would send information to one another via Facebook messages instead of typical forms of communication like texting or emailing. It went on for about a month and a half before I went back to visit her to see if we could have an actual offline relationship.

"Mind you, at this point I had real feelings for her. I'm not sure if it was love, but it was close. But after we reconnected in person, she said that we didn't have any chemistry. After that, our Facebook communication essentially tapered off until there was almost nothing left.

"Now, although she may not respond to emails or text messages or even Facebook messages, she'll always return a poke. A poke is OK. It means 'I know you're there, and I don't have to talk to you, but I am at least acknowledging that you exist.

"There's a poke outstanding on my page now. You can't turn the things off. You have to reply back...but I haven't replied back. I hope she sees that I'm ignoring her weak attempt at communication.

"This is how I see it. In computer terms, a thousand kilobytes equals a megabyte of information. When you send a message via Facebook, you're sending less than a thousand kilobytes. Even if you receive a long letter, it's probably not going to add up to a megabyte. I'm not worth the effort of typing even a few hundred kilobytes or a simple 'Hello, hope you're OK.' I'm worth the button that you can press to avoid talking to me."

CHAPTER 28:

WHY WON'T HE SAY HE'S 'IN A RELATIONSHIP?'

It's sad but true that the relationship status section on Facebook has been known to end many a (somewhat decent) relationship.

Most men absolutely refuse to commit online, while the women in their lives are perplexed, stunned and pissed off that their men won't make it official…on Facebook or otherwise.

There are several different relationship status options on the old 'Book. Under the "About Me" section, you can be: single, in a relationship, in an open relationship, engaged, married, it's complicated, widowed or opt for nothing at all.

I'm going to put it right out there…if you've been sleeping with someone and his status still says 'single', you might have to reassess your (lack of a) relationship.

It's possible that he just isn't aware of his status, but I'd only use that excuse if he barely uses the site or has a job that doesn't involve a computer.

I expect someone in advertising or sales to be far more cognizant of what's happening online than, say, a chef (celebrity chefs who appear on reality series don't count). Still, it's pretty much a given that a man who lists himself as single feels very much the same way.

It's preferable if his status gives nothing way, meaning that he's removed the 'relationship' option from his page completely. Essentially, he's following the advice his mom gave him as a kid: say something nice or nothing at all. By not claiming himself as a swinging singleton or a taken man either way, he isn't pressured to offer up information or incur your wrath if you happen to be dating him.

After all, if you're seriously dating it *is* within your rights to protest the 'single' relationship status on his page, but if he doesn't put it out there at all you might not have much of a leg to stand on.

It's only fair that your Facebook status reflects that you *are* in a real relationship, if it's that important to you. You aren't crazy to request that other women know your man is off the market.

However, you *might* be crazy if you rush him into making this sort of online commitment. Just because you've gone on a couple of dates with a guy doesn't mean he's your boyfriend. Heck, just because you've been seeing him for three months doesn't mean it's a done deal! Each couple is different, and everyone moves at their own pace.

An example: My friend Leann was dating a co-worker. They both worked in a prison, and decided to avoid job-related conflicts by leaving their statuses blank. To hear her tell it, their relationship was fine, so I was shocked to hear that they broke up relatively quickly after having a discussion about the ol' Facebook relationship status. As it turned out, though they had a mutual respect for one another, they both agreed that their relationship was never completely *right*. It's funny that having a Facebook-related discussion about the seriousness of their situation made them both realize they weren't a fit.

Unfortunately, most of these discussions don't turn out as smoothly as Leann's did. A woman often pushes the man until he reveals the real reason behind his hesitation in saying he's part of a couple is that he, in fact, *isn't* and furthermore, *doesn't want to be*. So leave your delusions behind and find someone who *wants* to be with you – and who isn't shy about admitting it to his 651 friends.

NATE'S STORY:
WHY I WOULDN'T SAY I WAS
'IN A RELATIONSHIP' ON FACEBOOK

"I don't like announcing to the world that I'm 'in a relationship' on Facebook. Let's put it this way: It's the difference between being in a prison (in a relationship) and being under house arrest (won't say either way). "This is a 'serious commitment' issue. A man thinks that when he says he's in a committed relationship on Facebook, he's one step away from getting engaged. Whereas if he doesn't commit online, he's one step away from freedom. Failing to put any kind of relationship status on your page is one way of saying you might still be looking for the next best thing, or that you just don't want to have any kind of conversation about your present relationship either way.

"I was seeing a girl named Hillary, and while the sex was good and I enjoyed being around her, I didn't want to be her boyfriend. Every time she started to have 'that' discussion, I quickly changed the topic. I liked spending time together, but I knew I didn't want to be committed to her. Once you have that 'commitment' talk, there's no way of going back – you're either in a relationship or you're breaking up.

"Needless to say, Hillary and I didn't last. Although she did try to have the relationship talk prematurely, I knew she wasn't the one for me. Trust me, if a guy wants to be with you, he'll make it known. That's why two months after I started dating Melissa, I didn't hesitate to declare my feelings to the Facebook world at large. She didn't even have to ask me to do it – I just wanted to.

So just a word of advice to all the single ladies out there: if he's not saying that he's with you on Facebook, he's *not* your boyfriend."

CHAPTER 29:

DOES A LACK OF ONLINE AFFECTION MATTER?

You've finally established that you're 'in a relationship' online, but he's refusing to leave adorable little love notes on your wall. The horror! Should you be royally ticked off that he doesn't feel the need to share how enamored of you he is the way you want him to, or do you let it go?

For heaven's sake ladies: LET IT GO. A man that's constantly leaving 'gifts' on your wall or writing "Baby, I love you. Kiss kiss" looks like a sucker. You have officially taken away his manhood, and that's not something to be proud of. You want a man, not a Mouseketeer, for cripes sake.

If he's being that gushy in real life, you've got a stage five clinger on your hands. Sooner or later, you *will* get sick of his mushiness (unless you yourself are equally that mushy, upon which I must tell you to reign in your sappy, cloyingly sweet behavior or someone might slap you).

Conversely, if he's only being sweet online and gives you totally adorable virtual flowers instead of the real deal, well then, that's just sad. Some men don't know better, but your guy is giving you some important information here. He's telling you that he realizes a bouquet of roses is a good idea, but that he's too cheap to purchase the real deal. Ouch.

Given that you haven't completely destroyed his manhood (yet), I'm sure you want to know *why* he isn't playing ball by writing on your wall. There are a variety of reasons, but the primary one is that men would rather show you how they feel then write it on some stupid social networking site (their words, not mine). Most use Facebook as a networking tool or as something to do when they're bored; they're not as religious about using it as girls are. To be honest, most men aren't even thinking about the love/relationship aspects of Facebook. That's all in *your* (and my) head.

Unfortunately, another reason they may not be writing on your wall is that they aren't as committed as you think. They may not want all of their female 'friends' – some of whom may be past hookups or ex-girlfriends – to see that they're so in to you. It's one thing for you to write on their wall – you could be any old girl, after all – and quite another for them to reciprocate.

Let's look at Ted and Ellen's situation. Ted is mostly a good guy, and he's completely in to Ellen, who's much younger than he is. She's an innocent, he's a bit more jaded.

Ellen can't stop leaving adorable little proclamation's on Ted's Facebook wall, including photographs of the two kissing and little notes reading "I love you! Have a great day!" Ted never responds or writes to Ellen on Facebook, but he constantly calls, texts and sees her.

He did admit to me, however, that Ellen's little declarations of love bother him. He says he's afraid of upsetting his ex-girlfriends, though I somewhat get the sense that he's actually worried about upsetting *future* girlfriends.

Men.

Keep in mind, these are worst-case scenarios. Your guy probably isn't sharing his affection on Facebook because he's not an avid user or because he thinks it's lame. If the latter is the case, power to him, and power to you for actually picking a guy who's sensible enough to realize that life outside of Facebook does exist! I just can't picture it, though. Can you?

CHAPTER 30:

THE EX-FACTOR – IF YOU BREAK UP, WHAT SHOULD YOU DO?

Breaking up is hard to do for a reason: it hurts. If it *didn't* hurt, we'd attach a fluffier, less harmless adverb to it.

That said, it sucks when a relationship goes wrong. Heading to splitsville is modern times is especially difficult, thanks, in part, to Facebook.

It definitely doesn't help you to heal if you're constantly confronted with reminders of not just the relationship you had, but of his/her very existence. If you haven't deleted your ex as a friend, he or she is still tagged in umpteenth photographs and you're still stuck seeing their status updates in your news feed.

So do you de-friend your former loves and put your pride on the line, or do you suffer in silence, hoping that you'll meet someone new one day soon and your heartbreak will lessen?

The de-friending process comes down to one thing: whether or not you intend to remain real-life friends (and not just cyber pals) with your ex, or if you think that moving on would be a healthier move in the long run. Be honest with yourself now. Although you might start off with the best intentions, sometimes it's easier to just say goodbye and get on with your life.

If you legitimately believe you can and will be friends again one day, then suck it up and try your best to avoid looking at his or her page. Thanks to the new privacy settings, it's possible that you can remove your ex from appearing in your news feed. Problem solved! Now it's up to you to avoid your curious urges, which you really, really should, because you might not like what you see if you go snooping.

If you take a long, hard look at your former relationship and realize that staying in touch won't benefit your or your mental health, then by all means, cut the cord and click the delete button.

If the breakup is especially painful and you still don't want to hurt the other person, you can always block him or her from seeing your page; it will appear as if you've cancelled your account. If you don't care, let the chips fall where they may. At least you won't be putting yourself through misery by constantly hitting the refresh button to see if they've posted anything new.

Look at it this way: if you've been dumped, why does your ex deserve the privilege of even having your online friendship? If he or she has anything to say about your *virtual* dumping (he won't, she might) you can always retort: "Sorry, honey, it's not you...it's me." Message received.

In case you still haven't made your decision, here's some additional food for thought: think about how you'll feel when you see that your ex has moved on and that their new squeeze is already blowing up all over their wall. I'll tell you this much: it isn't going to feel good. It's already broken, but pain on top of pain is still pain.

ANNA'S STORY: HE DELETED ME AS A FACEBOOK FRIEND

"Dave and I had been dating for almost a year and a half, and try as I might to make it work, it never felt completely right. I always felt slightly uncomfortable with him, like when you're lying in bed with someone and you don't know where to put your arm, so you let him sleep on it, and it's not a good feeling for either of you.

"I wasn't in love with him, but I liked him a lot. I guess I was determined to stay with him because I was ready for a relationship and he seemed, on paper, like the perfect partner.

263

"But he wasn't perfect by any means. He'd 'forget' to call during a weekend away with his friends and disappear during the week for days, only to reemerge with a text saying, 'Hey, let's do dinner.' I couldn't take it anymore, so I decided to have 'the conversation.' Only, I chickened out before I could say anything – but he didn't. Nope, he was more than brave enough to end it.

"For some reason – probably because the masochistic part of me feels like because I didn't end it, I'm now the one holding on – I couldn't let go. I was pathetic. I cried and sniffled and said, 'We'll still be friends, right?' He didn't say anything, but he hugged me really tightly, so I took his silence as agreement.

"Big mistake. The next day I woke up, went to work and decided to indulge in a little bit of Facebook stalking, just to see if he was at all mourning my loss as I was mourning his. Only, I couldn't see anything on his page at all: the bastard had de-friended me. Although my head knew that he and I weren't right and that he never treated me the way I deserved to be treated, it was still a shock.

"When we parted ways, I really thought he would still somehow be in my life, that I could slowly wean myself off of him. I'm a good person, and I've never had anyone defriend me before. I couldn't believe that someone I'd cared so much about for the last year would be callow and immature enough to completely shut me out.

"In hindsight, I'm glad that I couldn't see what he was up to. I couldn't check up on him or obsess about whether or not he was already dating. As it happened, he moved on *much* faster than I did. Had I been able to access his page, I would have seen that he started dating someone new less than two months after we ended things. Having to find out about his new girlfriend through a mutual friend was embarrassing, but I'd much rather suffer a little mortification that have to see the evidence that I was so inconsequential on a daily basis."

ASHLEY'S STORY: I KEPT HIM AS A FACEBOOK FRIEND

"I had only been dating my boyfriend for about a year, but I really thought it was love. I've never been one of those girls who dreamed about her fantasy wedding or who sighed every time she saw a wedding dress, but I actually thought 'he's the one: *this* is the man I'm going to marry.' It was intense.

"Ben and I certainly weren't without our share of problems, though. I was never 100% confident in our relationship. I knew that he had issues with intimacy, but I thought that by being there for him and giving him his space, he would finally realize that he couldn't ever be without me. I got all romantic about it. I wanted to be his air.

"During the earliest days of our relationship, he was away a lot. He frequently traveled for work, and while he was away I would keep tabs on him by checking his Facebook page almost obsessively.

"Sure, I knew this wasn't healthy, and I eventually stopped when I realized that I was starting to get jealous over every single harmless comment any female wrote on his wall. I didn't like that someone who was supposed to make me so happy always ended up making me feel bad – through little fault of his own, I might add.

"If I'm being honest, it wasn't other women I was worried about – I knew he wouldn't cheat. It was the fundamental flaws that were always present in our relationship from day one: the way he always kept me at a distance, as if he were saying hello and goodbye all at the same time, our values, our different interests. At the end, I ultimately decided that we couldn't really build a life together, though I still couldn't let go because I loved him.

"By the time we broke up, it was almost a relief to hear him say that he didn't love me anymore. I was initially sad, and then I got mad – he had never told me he loved me in the first place. To hear that he had after a year of being together and just hadn't shared it made me feel bereft, like I had lost something important.

"This anger gave me fuel. I realized that, had he really loved me, he would have told me so. He had used that to hurt me, like a weapon.

"I know that it's not mature, but I thought the best way of getting revenge would be to see how quickly I moved on. I constantly posted pictures of myself looking fabulous on Facebook, posing with this guy or that guy. I wanted him to realize that losing me was a failure on his part, and that I was a hot commodity that he had lost forever.

"So, although I couldn't resist checking up on him after our break-up for a bit, I'm glad I didn't de-friend him. Though I may not be the bigger person inside (and clearly am not because I insist on playing these petty games), I still *looked* like I was by being mature by keeping him in my Facebook life, despite having effectively ex'd him out of the real thing. And for the record, I know my updates were driving him insane. Yes, satisfaction is keeping me warm at night."

CHAPTER 31:

CAN FACEBOOK-RELATED JEALOUSY RUIN MY RELATIONSHIP?

We've already discussed how it can problematic if we obsessively compulsively check out our ex's Facebook page for evidence that he or she has moved on. But a new study has made the entirely valid claim that Facebook also increases jealousy while you're *in* a functional relationship.

Jealousy causes us to act in ways and do things we didn't think we were capable of doing. Whitney Houston revealed her justified paranoia in "It's Not Right, But It's OK, singing: "Friday night you and your boys went out to eat then you hung out, but you came home around three. If six of y'all went out, then four of you were really cheap 'cause only two of you had dinner, I found your credit card receipt."

If rooting through your guy's pockets isn't something you'd normally do, then the green-eyed monster has definitely bitten you...and you're not alone. According to a study published in the *CyberPsychology & Behavior Journal*[36] "increased Facebook use significantly predicts Facebook-related jealousy" in romantic relationships.

Two hundred thirty one college women were surveyed, answering questions ranging from "How likely are you to monitor your partner's activities on Facebook?" to "How likely are you to become jealous after your partner has added an unknown member of the opposite sex?"

The study had some interesting results -- 19.1% of the girls polled discovered they became more jealous when they had easy access to their boyfriend's every move; 16.2% of the women blamed Facebook, 10.3% of the women couldn't control themselves from constantly checking what their man was up to. Yet only 7.4% seemed to understand that their actions might be causing unnecessary problems where none existed.

So what do you do about the green-eyed monster? You always have options, you know. You can suffer silently, you can drive yourself crazy by making up fake scenarios in your head or you can actually track his or her actions like a bunny boiler.

Monitoring tools like Stealth IBot do exist these days. If you're super paranoid about what he's doing, you can buy this nifty tracking device,

••••••••••••••••••••••••
36 *Parr, Ben.* August 9 2009.< http://mashable.com/2009/08/09/facebook-relationship-jealous/>.

which records all activities on all types of web accounts, including Facebook. It can even save up to 10,000 screenshots as "evidence" of how your respective other spends his or her time.

Personally, I think that the more you give in to your jealousy, the crazier it will make you. Call it a day, realize you're making a mountain out of a molehill and try to focus on what you could be accomplishing if you weren't wasting all of your time and energy creating problems where none exist.

MEGAN'S STORY

"I've been dating my boyfriend, Ryan, for about a year now and I'm not ashamed to say that he actually deleted his Facebook page because he couldn't deal with my jealousy.

"To be fair to me, it only happened once that I lit into him about a girl who was posting on his wall. I was like, 'Who *is* this slut posting on you wall?' He couldn't take my jealousy, so he deleted the account all on his own.

"He never really used it much anyway, but I'm a huge Facebook user and I would tag him in posts and pictures all the time. His friends would constantly give him grief, but I never really assumed that it bothered him because he never untagged himself from anything.

"I mean, they made fun of him a *lot*. There was a major issue when I put up 'in a relationship' and he accepted the change on his page. His friends definitely had some negative thoughts on the matter – I don't really think they're fans of me – but I never got to read exactly what they said because he deleted the comments right away. He kept the 'in a relationship' status up though, for as long as he was actually on Facebook.

"He lasted for another five months before I started with the questions, and then he just straight up deleted his account. Even though I can't tell the world who it is I'm in a relationship with, I still let everyone know that I'm a taken woman."

CHAPTER 32:

HOW DO I USE THE NEW TIMELINE TO HIDE MY SHADY PAST?

As if Facebook weren't already complicated enough, Mark Zuckerberg and his merry band of computer-friendly social networkers decided to add yet another complicated feature to this hugely popular site: the Timeline.

The Timeline could be the bane of your existence if you don't learn how to use it properly. Every single post you've ever created since the first, innocent day you joined Facebook will be available for all and sundry to see. That means that every drunken Facebook message you've ever posted from your cell phone and every sappy ode to your ex-boyfriend has not only returned from the grave of posts past, but they're all on full display. I think this deserves an "OMG," don't you?

Sorry to be the bearer of bad tidings, but I have more unfortunate news for you. Not only is it easy for you to scroll back in time to see the faux pas your younger self made online, but everyone else can see them, too. All they need to is go to a specific year on your profile and click the "All Posts" button.

This means that – for some of you – posts you wrote in *high school* will be visible, as were the braces, pimples and bad hair you also rocked back in the day. Have you just gone as white as a sheet? I know I did when I looked back at some of my photos…

I wish, wish, wish I had good news for you, but alas, I don't. You're going to have to scroll back through every single post you ever wrote and click "Hide from Timeline" using the pencil icon, or you're going to have to choose "Friends Only" as your privacy setting. This, too, is problematic if you only share certain posts with certain friends. Still, it's better than nothing. To do this, head to Privacy Settings and then select "Limit the Audience for Past Posts." You'll then click on "Limit Old Posts" after pressing the button that says "Manage Past Post Visibility."

Unless you're prepared to individually go back through every single one of your old posts, you're leaving yourself wide open for a curious new boyfriend or a potential suitor with a extra time on his hands to rifle through your uncensored past. For 99.9% of the 845 million Facebook users in the world, that picture isn't going to be entirely pretty.

Conversely, you're also going to have to remember those relationships you wish you could block out (which you were able to do until the Timeline reared its ugly head in December of 2011, that is). Your exes will start cropping up all like wildfire, so you might want to avoid overanalyzing your past for a while.

You also could pretend that the Timeline is like one, gigantic time capsule that someone dug up early and put on display in Times Square. Your past is there for the perusing, but will your new loves be cataloguing each and every little thing you've ever done?

My fingers are crossed for each and every one of you (and myself) that the answer is "NO."

CHAPTER 33:

WHAT SHOULD I DO IF I'VE FRIENDED HIM AND CAN'T RESIST STALKING HIS PAGE?

Befriending a guy that you actually have a hope of dating is pretty much the worst thing you can ever do – on Facebook, that is. Sorry, but I've said it – and it's true. Very few of us can resist the temptation to check out his status updates to see what he's feeling, to see who he's become friends with (especially if they're female) and reading comments posted by others to see what he's doing.

Accepting a guy you want to date is a recipe for disaster, and not just because you know you'll have the tendency to 'stalk' his every move. No, he'll be able to see what *you* have been up to, and, based on what he's reading, he might make some incorrect assumptions about who you are and what you're looking for.

Unfortunately, it's almost a prerequisite in modern relationships that you Facebook one another before you even call each other on the phone

(Phone calls? Who *does* that anymore?). Alas, it seems like it's here to stay, so if you insist on becoming his Facebook friend before you're actually even dating, you need to know how avoid screwing up your blossoming relationship from the get-go.

First off, I know it's hard, but please try to exercise some willpower. Limit your 'casual' checks to one quick scan per day. Try not to read too much into everything he writes, and don't assume everything is about you. If you're in the initial stages of dating, remember that he *is* allowed to see other women until you've made it exclusive, as you're allowed to see other men. Don't freak.

If there are those of you who have admirably restrained from even glancing at his page, but are seduced into taking a peek when he comes up in your news feed, here's yet another trick: you can unsubscribe from him! Yes, it's true. All you need to do is go to his page (one last time, ladies, one last time) and click on the "subscribe" button, changing it to "unsubscribe." It's that simple.

Next, for your own security, put him on a limited profile setting so that he can only see *some* of the shenanigans you've been up to. That said, because of the new security settings, you now have the ability to censor what he sees, so be vigilant about it. If you're going to play the game while using social media, you might as well play it smart.

This goes for photos, too. You might (and by "might" I mean *should*) want to go back and keep him from seeing certain albums. You don't want to give any guy that you're serious about dating the idea that you're a good-time girl, that you have a problem with alcohol or can't seem to stop sticking your tongue down the throats of strange men. Then again, if you're constantly making out with random guys, you have other things to worry about than what one dude thinks of your Facebook profile. Just saying.

CHAPTER 34:

DO PEOPLE ACTUALLY DUMP THEIR PARTNERS ON FACEBOOK?

Picture this: The sun is shining, the birds are singing and you've just woken up. It's a glorious day! You're happy, you're in love, you're raring to go out there and show the world what you can do!

But first, you sign on to your Facebook page and realize that while you were sleeping (or showering) the status that just yesterday read "in a relationship" now reads: "Kristen is no longer in a relationship with Jay." You have just discovered that you have been *dumped* by your boyfriend of five months, and that he was heartless enough to do so on Facebook first, without even talking to you.

You may not know someone it's happened to (and cross your fingers that you never do), but it shouldn't come as a surprise to anyone that Facebook is an easy place to quickly and effectively end a relationship.

If you need reasons, here they are. Not only can you avoid a confrontation with your soon-to-be-ex, but you can also immediately cut them out of your life by de-friending them. Nothing says 'I want you gone' like deleting them as a Facebook friend. It's like, *way* harsh.

But the statistics speak for themselves. Market research firm Lab 42 determined that 33% of their respondents[37] had dumped someone via Facebook or text, while an additional 40% said they hadn't done so yet…but that they would. Cold-hearted snakes, you lot! Facebook dating app AreYouInterested also conducted a study, which also indicates that Facebook has become the easy way out of a disintegrating or unappealing relationship.[38]

Are you ready for a sad, shocking statistic? Twenty-five percent of respondents found out their relationship was over by seeing it on Facebook first. Meaning: instead of having a mature, adult, face-to-face conversation, your boyfriend's relationship status suddenly reads "single" instead of "in a relationship." And he didn't even give you the "It's not you, it's me" talk first. The horror!

••••••••••••••••••••••••

37 *Daily Mail Online.* November 14, 2011. <http://www.dailymail.co.uk/news/article-2061492/Faulty-connection-Third-people-broken-Facebook-email-text.html>.

38 AreYouInterested study http://mashable.com/2010/06/21/facebook-break-up/

Unsurprisingly, 70% of this particular survey's participants were men. But then, men are much more likely than women to avoid an emotional confrontation at all costs – and to be far more ruthless when dealing with the end of a relationship.

But back to the bad business of breaking up over Facebook, which isn't just disrespectful, but completely cowardly and un-cool. It's apparently become such a common problem that the Boston Public Health Commission even sponsored a one-day conference on "healthy breakups" in 2011.[39]

Sure, the conference attendees were mostly adolescents, but learning the ropes of respect at a young age is, in my book, a good thing. Some 200 teenagers gathered to discuss "creating online boundaries" and assess the difference between a "healthy" (Cameron Diaz and Justin Timberlake shooting a film together after their split) and "unhealthy" breakup (Sammi "Sweetheart" de-friending Ronnie's friends on Facebook after one of their many breakups.) They also taught the teens to avoid using social media or texts to do the dirty work they should be bravely doing in person.

To that I say one thing and one thing only: AMEN.

••••••••••••••••••••••••
39 *Denizet-Lewis, Enoit.* August 3, 2011. <http://www.nytimes.com/2011/08/07/magazine/teaching-kids-how-to-break-up-nicely.html?_r=2>.

PART V:

THE DANGERS OF FACEBOOK

CHAPTER 35:

FAKE FACEBOOK PROFILES

Facebook is all about showcasing who you are, what you like and where you've been. It's basically a gigantic scrapbook of what you've done in your life. That said, it's pretty hard to imagine someone creating a fake profile, right? Wrong.

I'm going to start right off the bat here with one of my beloved scenarios. Envision this: you're on Facebook for the nineteenth time in one day. All of a sudden, you have a friend request from a *very* sexy gentleman who is totally and completely foreign to you. He hasn't written a message, just sent a friend request. Because you aren't yet "friends," you can't see his profile – but you're flattered as all hell that this model perfect man wants to be *your* friend.

So you accept. He seems legit, despite having very few photos. Also, it appears to only be women posting on his wall, writing things like, "Hey sexy. That's a good look for you!" or "Hey lover, hope you're having a dandy day! Hearts and kisses, Candy."

"He's a player," you think dismissively, and go about your business. You forget to put him on a privacy filter because, well, what harm could it do if he saw *all* of your photos? He thought you were cute enough to friend you in the first place, didn't he? And he doesn't even know you, so what could really go wrong?

Bet you don't know what you did by ignorantly befriending a total stranger, do you? Sorry, love, but you've just given your ex-boyfriend (or his jealous new girlfriend) free reign to see who and what you're doing.

That's right, the fake profile does exist, and you have been duped – which is a heck of a lot different from being punk'd Ashton Kutcher-style.

These faux profiles are cropping up more and more, and aren't always considered to be harmless. A Moroccan man, Fouad Mortada, was sentenced to three years in prison and a $1,000 fine after claiming to be a Moroccan prince. English businessman Matthew Firsht won $43,767 in damages against an old school friend who put libelous and unauthorized information about him on Facebook. College students in Cambridge, England were also dismayed to find that their Facebook pal Pedro Amigo was actually their dean, Peter Linehan, who was spying on them after they formed a protest group to complain about a change in drinking laws.

It's frightening how easy it is to create a faux profile. All you need is an email address, which is nearly as easy to procure as air these days. Steal some sexy, fake shots from a model's portfolio online or something from Google images, and voila! You're ready to start your voyeuristic new life.

If this freaks you out beyond belief, you need to realize that it *could* happen to you. I could tell you that you shouldn't accept every Tom, Dick and Harry that asks to be your buddy, but that could be wasted breath. Some people just like having a lot of Facebook friends; it makes them feel popular. But with all the new privacy settings on Facebook today, it's very easy to restrict the strangers so being your "friend" will frustratingly get them absolutely nowhere.

You should automatically be putting people you don't know and/or don't trust on both restricted and limited access as soon as you accept them. This way, they won't be able to view your photos or your wall posts. Also remember, you can always see the way that any of your friends view your profile, so test it out just to be safe.

Otherwise, be wary of these signs that indicate you're about to become a victim of the fake profile:

1) A model-perfect stranger of the opposite sex (or same sex) is attempting to befriend you.

You have never seen him/her before in your life.

2) A celebrity has added you.

3) If you do add the person and realize they have three or less photographs up, you're being taken for a ride.

4) Again, if you've befriended, quickly take a look at their wall. If it appears that none of their friends have actually met him/her, you should probably delete this new friendship immediately.

5) The person in question has a completely public profile and has not been tagged by anyone else.

Be smart.

KEITH'S STORY:
AN EXPLANATION OF WHY I CREATED
A FAKE FACEBOOK PROFILE

"The idea behind creating a fake profile started because of an annoying guy who started to "like" every single one of my girlfriend Tamara's status updates. If she wrote "I'm going to the grocery store" or "I like cats" or even something cliched like, "Live like there's no tomorrow," Eric would like it. I was angry. I would think to myself, "Who is the jerk constantly commenting on *my* girlfriend's posts?"

"When I finally asked her about it, she said she didn't even know who he was. She told me he was a guy who had friended her and she thought she knew him from years past but was wrong. I thought it was weird that she didn't just delete him if she didn't know him, and began to get suspicious. Then I saw a text message between the two of them and I knew she had lied to me. I thought, "I need to find out who this guy is, and I want to catch her in a lie."

"So I created the fake profile, and I was smart about it. When you're creating a fake profile, you have to invent an email address, so I made up something innocuous. I took a profile photo off of a Russian singles marriage arrangement website and made sure the girl was attractive but not ridiculously hot. I gave her an Arizona address, made her from a different country – an expat with a green card. I was vague about the details. When you're inventing a person, you want to make sure he or she can't be traced.

"I started to friend businesses first, then build up from there. I figured, if you're going to get a friend request from someone who has two friends, you're not going to accept or you're going to get suspicious. Then I looked at the person I wanted to become friends with – Eric – and looked at his friends list. I then started friending the companies and businesses he had listed as friends. I began to create the blueprint for a profile by populating my page with general status updates. Then, I friended the friends I thought would accept. When in doubt, go for the people that don't look very intelligent or that look like they'd friend anyone, like a shirtless guy on a motorbike showing off his tattoos in his profile picture or an attractive girl with 3,000 friends who writes status updates every hour. It really is fascinating how many people accept friend requests from people they don't know.

"Then came the moment of truth. I had my profile, a couple of weeks of status updates and over 100 friends (under 100 still looks of sketchy). I friend requested Eric, the guy I wanted to spy on, and he accepted. It was almost too easy.

"I found out that my gut intuition was right: Tamara *was* lying to me and she *did* know him. She was commenting on and liking his status updates almost as much as he had been liking hers. As it turned out, she was having an affair with a completely different person though at least I was right that she was a liar.

"Incidentally, she *did* end up dating Eric, or sleeping with him, at least. They'd both upload photographs or check in on Foursquare at the same bar at the same time, though never together.

"I realize that I was a little paranoid in this situation, but I had a gut feeling that something was wrong with my relationship and I wanted to get to the bottom of it. I did question the morality of it. I thought, "Am I doing the right thing?" I still feel a little bad about it, but I would have felt worse if I hadn't found anything. I would have felt paranoid and poorly about myself as someone who needed to create a fake profile to check up on his girlfriend. I would have thought, "What has this person done to me and my character that has led me to spy?"

"But in hindsight, I'm glad I created that profile. I still might've been pursuing a relationship that was unhealthy for me. It gave me peace of mind and saved me aggravation.

"The way I see it is this: dating is like a job. If you're going into an interview at Goldman Sachs, the head of HR isn't going to say, 'He's a good person, so let's hire him.' They're going to do background checks because they're investing a lot of time and money on an employee. Dating is the same kind of thing. I needed to check to make sure my ex was the person she said she was.

"I've always prided myself on being a good judge of character. I failed miserably with Tamara. I thought she was a good person; she wasn't. Never in my life have I been around someone that lies that badly or is that manipulative. So if you have similar suspicions, a fake profile might be a good call, because she won't be giving you a list of references.

"The most important job anybody is trying out for in a life is that of being someone's life partner. That's the most important "job interview" you have. Sometimes it just requires doing due diligence."

CHAPTER 36:

FACEBOOK, HOME TO THE MODERN-DAY CHEATER

Facebook is a blessing in so many ways, but it can also be a curse. Connecting with new people and reconnecting with old friends – old *flames* in particular – can sometimes make you forget that who you have in the present is more important than the loves you've gotten over in the past.

By friending an ex-boyfriend or girlfriend, you're lulled into reliving the good old days. Rarely will you remember that the relationship in question wasn't as perfect as you would have liked, or that it ended badly for a reason. What you will think is "What if this person is the one that got away?" This is especially problematic if you happen to currently be married or in a committed relationship.

Facebook cheating does tend to mostly affect relationships that are already rocky. It can also happen to someone who wants to escape his or her reality – if they've recently lost a job, are stressed out by work or are exhausted by the unglamorous rigors of caring for a young child – by losing themselves in the fantasy of an ex or the hope of new, uncharted territory.

This sort of infidelity can literally affect anyone. Actress Eva Longoria is living proof. The diminutive former *Desperate Housewives* star seemed to be desperately in love with her NBA player husband Tony Parker, until, of course, she found out that he had been unfaithful not once, but *twice*, during their four-year marriage. Though their relationship disintegrated after she discovered hundreds of texts between her now-ex and his then-teammate's wife, Longoria admitted that he had also cheated on her earlier in their marriage with an ex he found on Facebook.

Though Parker got busted, Facebook is, quite, literally, a cheater's playground. All you need do is erase your newly added "friend" from your Timeline, block your partner from seeing your friends and block your ex from seeing your relationship status. Additionally, you can restrict your ex from posting on your wall and correspond with he/she via email, which won't be visible to anyone.

Facebook might just be the "portal to infidelity" a New Jersey pastor claims it is. Rev. Cedric Miller made headlines for urging his congregation to delete their accounts after 20 couples confessed that Facebook had caused them to cheat.

While the web can take away, it can give back, too. Support group sites like marriagehelper.com offer assistance for the victims of online cheaters. Then there's FacebookCheating.com, a site that gives tips on how to catch a cheating spouse – and allows you to post your own bitter little tales of love. Revengeisadishbestservedcold.com, anyone?

MICHAELA'S STORY:
I FOUND OUT MY BOYFRIEND
WAS CHEATING VIA FACEBOOK

"I found out my boyfriend's Facebook password while we were dating, but I swore I'd never use it. But I couldn't prevent my best friend from writing it down for me. She told me, 'You need to keep this.'

"We were doing the long-distance thing while he was living in China for the year, talking virtually every day by phone, Skype or email. Though Chris seemed like the perfect boyfriend, there was one small snag in our relationship: he refused to change his Facebook relationship status from 'single' to 'in a relationship.' It didn't begin to bother me until my friend, who was constantly in my ear, demanded over and over again to know *why* he wouldn't change it. I didn't have an answer.

"One day he posted an album and I kept repeatedly seeing pictures of Chris posing with a girl – a girl who was really, really cute. I hadn't been worried about him living in Asia for a year. Our relationship was solid, and I didn't think there would be much of an opportunity for him to meet women, but then I began to notice how often 'Becky' was posting on his wall.

"I simmered and stewed about it until one day I just overflowed. I wrote him an email, telling him that I was at the end of my rope. I was vague, but also insistent, telling him, 'Things have to change'. Needless to say, he called me immediately.

"He made an excuse, of course. He told me that he was nervous about putting those photographs up on Facebook because he knew 'what I would think.' I was like, 'really? If you know I was going to think it, why did you still do it?' But I ignored that voice and listened to him tell me that he had posted the shots because he thought they were artistic, that she was only one of his friends and that he was lonely in a *Lost in Translation* kind of way, so shouldn't he make all the friends he possibly could?

"I made the executive decision to get over it; I chose to believe him. But then the photo comments started coming and his Facebook friends kept saying what a cute couple he and Becky made. I was furious. He and I were a couple, not some random girl he met in China! I had to get to the bottom of the situation.

"So I did what I promised myself I would not do. I logged onto his Facebook account and read the messages he and Becky had sent to one another. To my relief, there was nothing there that would indicate that he had lied to me.

"But it was like an addiction. I couldn't stop logging onto his account and reading his private messages to find out what was going on behind the scenes. And then one day proved all my suspicions right and rendered all my spying necessary.

"Chris' best friend in the States had just been to visit him in China. Bobby wrote him a lengthy Facebook message, talking about how gorgeous Becky was, how much he liked her and how great they were together. I, of course, was not mentioned at all.

"Because I wanted to make sure I could say everything I needed to say, I wrote him another email instead of calling. I said, 'I'm giving you one last chance to be honest with me. Tell me the truth, are you cheating on me?' He wrote back this long, three-page email which was honest to a point that it made me uncomfortable. At first he was like, 'How dare you say this to me?' but he quickly changed gears. He told me that nothing ever happened between he and Becky, that she was 'like a sister' to him. He then listed pages full of personal secrets that I really didn't need or want to know about in a bid to prove to me that he was honest. In hindsight, I realized that he was overcompensating to avoid the real issue at hand.

"Despite his heartfelt letter, the messages about his relationship with Becky kept popping up on Facebook, and I began to have a meltdown. When he called me acting all sweet and nice from China one day, the only words I would say to him were, 'I know what's going on.' He hung up on me.

"Needless to say, our relationship deteriorated completely from that point on. We had a huge, devastating breakup (devastating for me, that is) just as he was heading back to the States. Becky, apparently, came with him and they immediately went off on a long, romantic vacation together. How do I know? I saw the pictures on Facebook. He was the love of my life, so of course I had to defriend him, especially because it seemed like he was rubbing his relationship with Becky in my face. He knew I would see their photos. He was being cruel.

"Chris never found out how I knew about his cheating. He thought it was one of his guy friends. I read the message he sent Bobby telling him so. He was pretty displeased that I dared to defriend him, though. He didn't 'get' why I would do such a thing.

"To this day Chris never admits that he cheated on me. And to this day, I don't feel badly about checking up on him, either. His blatant lies were ten thousand times grosser than the fact that I went behind his back to check up on my completely untrustworthy boyfriend."

CHAPTER 37:

THE FACEBOOK-RELATED DIVORCE FACTOR

Ready for a shocker? If you've read the above title, you already know what I'm about to say, but that doesn't make the information any less sensational. New studies reveal that Facebook is responsible for the demise of *one in five* marriages.

According to a survey conducted by the American Academy of Matrimonial Lawyers (AAML),[40] one third of splitting spouses use the social networking site as proof that they have legitimate cause to file for divorce. Sixty-six percent of those surveyed cited Facebook posts from their ex as evidence. MySpace and Twitter were also listed as evidence, though to lesser degrees.

AAML President Marlene Eskind Moses made the following statement: "Going through a divorce always results in heightened levels of personal

....
40 *American Academy of Matrimonial Lawyers.* February 10, 2010. <http://www.aaml.org/about-the-academy/press/press-releases/e-discovery/big-surge-social-networking-evidence-says-survey->.

scrutiny. If you publicly post any contradictions to previously made statements and promises, an estranged spouse will certainly be one of the first people to notice and make use of that evidence. As everyone continues to share more and more aspects of their lives on social networking sites, they leave themselves open to much greater examinations of both their public and private lives in these sensitive situations."

She's right: which is why I'm constantly preaching that you not make your public affairs – whether you're dating, in a relationship or simply trying to attract someone's attention – quite so public.

The British website Divorce-Online has taken their findings one step further to discern why, exactly, Facebook was being cited for 33 percent of all U.K. divorces in 2011. Of the 5000 people surveyed, three pieces of "evidence" kept cropping up: inappropriate messages sent to someone of the opposite sex, a spouse posting nasty comments about their ex on the site and Facebook "friends" reporting on the soon-to-be-ex's behavior.

Which goes to show – you can never be too cautious. Any problems that existed in the relationship were there already, but given that Facebook is such a public forum, even the end of love apparently, is interactive.

CHAPTER 38:

SUMMING IT UP

By now you understand that Facebook can make or break a relationship and that befriending the person you're interested (especially if you're a woman) can be detrimental to your sanity.

In case you've forgotten these key elements, here's a quick refresher course of all you need to know about using Mark Zuckerberg's social network to your benefit!

♥ Privacy settings are there for a reason and can get you out of some potentially sticky situations

♥ You're going to have to watch what you say even more than usual thanks to the new Timeline feature

♥ Leaving your relationship status blank is probably the best move you can make

♥ Don't update your statuses to reveal anything about who you're dating or what you're feeling

- ♥ Facebook stalkers and Facebook fakes do exist
- ♥ How to handle a breakup via Facebook
- ♥ Whether or not to defriend your ex
- ♥ Facebook is a great modern day tool for scoring dates

CHALLENGE: Though you desperately want to friend that girl or guy you're into, refrain for as long as possible or -- better yet -- don't do it at all. Ladies, if a guy really likes you, he should be contacting you the old-fashioned way: by phone. Gentlemen, are you listening?

SECTION 3:

OTHER TOOLS OF THE TRADE - TWITTER, FOURSQUARE, EMAIL & MYSPACE

PART I:

TWITTER

What *is* Twitter? Sorry, but if you still think that a tweet is a sound made by birds, you are so 1996.

Twitter is a social media platform where users share snippets of their thoughts in 140 characters or less. The site, created in 2006 by Jack Dorsey, first asked its users "What are you doing?" but changed its strategy to "What's happening?" in 2009 in order to receive a broader spectrum of responses.

As of late 2011, 300 million users had signed up for the site in order to share news, information and – yes – their own thoughts.

But will your shared thoughts get you into trouble in love? Can sharing anything at all, however small, be problematic?

CHAPTER 39:

TMI TROUBLE

Twitter seems relatively harmless. What's to fear? There are tiny blue birds in the background, and you can decorate your page in a variety of skins / rainbow-hued backgrounds that are so colorful they remind you of Willy Wonka's chocolate factory. Plus, how many problems can 140 measly characters create?

The answer: a whole slew, and then some.

Many problems can arise from airing your dirty laundry in such a public forum. The fact alone that you're comfortable enough giving strong snippets of your feelings for the world to see (unless your account is locked, which defeats the purpose of Twitter in general) is bad enough. But letting everyone know your very personal thoughts on an ongoing basis makes you the queen (or king) of TMI: Too Much Information.

The very best tweets are those from comedians like Sarah Silverman or Conan O'Brien. They're pithy, to the point and they make you laugh, cringe and nod in agreement at the same time.

Then there are those who share personal information about themselves, albeit in an amusing way. Actress Ellen Barkin in particular makes no excuses for who she is and still manages make the mundane look sexy online.

You *don't* want to be a Jennifer Love Hewitt or Leann Rimes, who tweet every time they go grocery shopping or get smooched. J. Love is especially bad, given that she's usually single. Her dreamy, love-obsessed Twitter feed is gag inducing and *will* scare off any man who happens to be reading. I envision Preston in *Can't Hardly Wait* shaking his head in pity and saying, "Man, Amandà Beckett is hot, but *way* too much drama. I don't want any part of that."

Telling the world your personal business on an ongoing basis is not only boring, but egotistical and self-absorbed. You wouldn't want these qualities in a man, so why should he enjoy them in you?

If you still need evidence that this obsessive desire to share every waking thought you have isn't necessarily a good thing, just look at the hot water that John Mayer got himself into on the social networking site.

He let his mansion-sized ego run amok, constantly tweeting arrogant fare like, "I love how some dudes hate me for dating their fantasy girl, as if they were going to if I hadn't" and "BREAKING CELEBRITY NEWS: I was sitting with my legs crossed for too long and my penis fell asleep."

When gems like "We all have a congenital hole in our heart. It comes down to how we go about filling it that matters" as well as some pissed off ex-girlfriends named Jennifer Aniston and Jessica Simpson caused the world to turn on old Johnny Boy, he deleted his Twitter account. Smooth move.

He explained his reasons while chatting to students from the Berklee College of Music, saying "I realized about a year ago that I couldn't have a complete thought anymore, and I was a tweeta-holic. I had four million Twitter followers, and I was always writing on it. I stopped using Twitter as an outlet and I started using Twitter as the in-strument to riff on, and it started to make my mind smaller and smaller and smaller. And I couldn't write a song."

So FYI, be wary of what you say and do on Twitter – it *will* come back to bite you in the behind.

WHY TWITTER GETS YOU IN TROUBLE: A TESTIMONIAL FROM THE MAN WHISPERER AUTHOR DONNA SOZIO

"Today, most first impressions aren't made in person: they are made online. Unlike when we meet face-to-face and slowly showing the other person our best selves, we air our dirty laundry in public every single time we Tweet.

"On first dates, it's rare that we reveal everything about ourselves at once. We wait until the other has fallen for us at our best before we slowly start to reveal our flaws. It's a good strategy, because by the time we've started to show our imperfect sides, our partner is equipped to love us instead of running for the hills.

"Twitter makes that slow reveal very, very tricky. We often use the site as a soapbox to draw a line in the sand, take a stand and shake our angry stick at hot button issues. We also tend to complain and rant about the little stuff that bugs us. We tweet to document our every waking thought and opinion, which, as it happens, can be quite negative at times. When it comes to dating, opinions -- especially strong ones -- can be a turn-off instead of a turn on. Our partner or partner-to-be can learn about our imperfections far more quickly and far easier than he might have otherwise.

"So make a promise to one another that you *will not* avidly read the other's Twitter feed in the early stages of your relationship. Get to know each other in person and in person only. Being an online enigma is only going to help you in the long run."

CHAPTER 40:

A LACK OF MYSTERY

"Be mysterious," John Bouvier told his daughter, Jacqueline. We all know what happened when she followed his advice. Jackie O was the lucky lady who got to get into bed with John F. Kennedy every night, became a fashion icon and was the tragic enigma of a bygone era. And – let me repeat this – she *married John F. Kennedy*.

A little mystery is essential in every relationship, which is why dating in the 21st century can be so difficult. The only 'mystery' you'll find nowadays is why someone *isn't* tweeting or posting about their every emotion.

These ongoing, bite-sized thoughts make it very possible for you to become a crashing bore. Twitter isn't your diary. People do read it. It's one thing to be true to who you are, and quite another to force your identity down people's throats.

Say that a guy you're into *does* check out your Twitter feed to see what you're all about. It isn't uncommon that he'd want to check up on a girl that he really likes, just as we ladies not so secretly scope out the men we like online. So he looks at your account. What is he going to find?

Is he going to see that you've gone all "Texts From Last Night" and have splattered your sex-ploitations across Twitter? Will he see that you're constantly moaning about being loveless a la sad singleton Bridget Jones? Or will your constant OMGS, BFFS and LOLS convince him that you're a pre-teen trapped in a 30-year-old's body?

As of 2011, Twitter created the following new mission statement: "To instantly connect people everywhere to what's most important to them."

Although it's a bit ambiguous in nature, you should still be aware that, though you are, of course, the most important person in your world, you never want to appear that way. Duh.

So start tweeting about the things you like as opposed to directly talking about yourself. When he goes to check out your page, he'll see that you've got interests and hobbies more impressive than a love of self.

CHAPTER 41:

DO NOT TWEET ABOUT YOUR SEX LIFE

I'm going to coin a term here, and it may not work. You'll see my point regardless. Talking about your sex life on Twitter is the online equivalent of a PDA. Hence, a TDA (Tweet Display of Affection) is born.

Is it coy and flirtatious to have two million followers (or thirty, I won't judge you) read about the naughty thing you did with your co-worker last night? Your readers might find it be funny, but your co-worker probably won't, nor will your boss, mother or the other guy you've been dating. In fact – dare I say it – you might look a little *slutty*.

I, for one, do not want to read about the amazing orgasm BlueEyedKitty7890 had last night, or that PetethePantherMan90210 gave it to her. Your sex life should remain between you and your partner, so by God, if you're going to talk about it over Twitter, at least send direct messages one another so those who follow you won't have to see it or want to gag.

If you need to engage in some online foreplay, for the love of all that is holy, do it in private!

While this is both a respect and a self-respect thing, a study by OKtrends [41]also proves that frequent tweeters have shorter real-life relationships than those who don't share their business with the world.

Sean Combs (otherwise known as Diddy) once discussed his sexual prowess *mid-session*. In a perfect world, the lady beneath him would have high-tailed it out there door when she saw him pick up his iPhone to write: "For all those just tuning in. I'm 6 and half hrs in on a 36-hour tantric sex session. Welcome."

Did she thank you?

Former U.S. rep Anthony Weiner would have had far less notoriety and a far calmer life if he had only kept his naked photographs – and his cheating – offline.

Ashton Kutcher and Demi Moore once used Twitter as foreplay – and despite the fact that they are both on Hollywood's hot list, didn't care who saw the evidence of their desire. Who can forget when they used a variety of Twitpics to play sexual hide-and-seek in their own home? For those

....
41 *Rudder, Christian.* April 19, 2011. <http://blog.okcupid.com/in-dex.php/10-charts-about-sex/>.

of you who aren't in the know, the *G.I. Jane actress* wrote "bed time?" on her chest. The *New Year's Eve* star's response: "4 sure." Demi then concluded their Twitter sexplay by writing on her hand: "Race you to the bedroom."

They are, of course, divorced now after he became another victim of "I can have it all" syndrome (aka he had Demi and his piece on the side, too).

The point here is that no matter which way you look at it, talking about sex isn't a smart thing when the sex life you're discussing is your own.

CHAPTER 42:

HAVE FAITH – ROMANCE CAN BLOSSOM IN THE TWITTERVERSE

Stranger things have happened than two people falling in love on the strength of several 140-character messages. Don't forget – love can happen anywhere, and when you least expect it.

That was the case when British television presenter Gregg Wallace met the woman he would eventually marry over the social networking site. The Masterchef host fell in love with Heidi Brown, one of his Twitter followers, in 2009 after she responded to his tweet of: "Jiggling cabbage is not a euphemism. No more than shuffling shallots or sorting celery." He gave the 17-years younger biology teacher from Northwest England a tweet-only lesson on celery sorting before writing: "Ever visit London? Give me a call, I'll buy you lunch." The rest, as they say, is history; the couple married in 2011.

But how do you make someone fall in love with you in less than fifty words? Well, it won't be easy, I'll give you that.

Ideally, you want to link up with people who like the same things you do. The easiest way to do this is to press the "Who to Follow" button and then browse by interest. In addition to looking for photos you might think are attractive, actually read the person's tweets and see if your have similar opinions or if the other person's Twitter posts make you laugh out loud (that's LOL, to those in the know). Then, send him/her an @ message with a question related to their post in order to spark a conversation.

For example, say you're into music and love the band Radiohead. BrandonForeverAndaDay has just tweeted that *Kid A* is the best album of all time. You're interested in Brandon based on the wit of his previous posts – although that cute little dimple in his left cheek doesn't hurt, either. What you want to do is send Brandon a pubic message showing that you actually a) have an opinion b) are capable of expressing that opinion and c) want to start a discussion about his statement. You might write something like, "I prefer *The Bends*, but would love to know your favorite track on *Kid A*. You've got good taste." Flattery *will* get you everywhere, my dears.

PART II:

EMAIL

I want to thank God for email – and at the same time, I want to say: "God, why in the world would you make it possible for guys to email girls in place of actual face-to-face or phone conversations?" Let me cut right to the chase and say that I loathe relationships where couples email one another on a regular basis. What was the cell invented for…just giggles?

While it is perfectly acceptable to write one another lengthy diatribes via Outlook, Gmail or Yahoo! while you're apart – in different cities, say – email should not become a substitute for the phone. That's weak.

I find that couples who frequently email one another rarely have anything interesting to say when they're face to face. If email is being used as an additional tool to furthering a relationship – to send cute pictures, or YouTube videos that your respective other might enjoy – that's OK. Just make sure you're not replacing actual contact with online contact.

It's also hard to gauge what someone means when you're emailing on the regular. You can easily take things out of context, misconstruing a joke for a serious, not altogether pleasant commentary on the state of your relationship.

Email is necessary, it is modern and it makes things easy – but, like the best things in life, the easiest things to catch aren't always the most worthwhile things to have.

CHAPTER 43:

WHAT YOU SHOULD BE SAYING IN PERSON

"I'm hungry."

"Really? Me too. I'm thinking about a cheeseburger."

"Really? I'm hungry for pizza. You should get a cheeseburger. Maybe I'll get pizza."

"Yeah. Maybe. But I'm kind of hungry for pizza too. There aren't any good places around here. So I'm kind of on the fence."

"You're right, you've got a tough decision. But I'm still going for pizza. By the way, what do you want to do tonight?"

"I don't know. What do you want to do?"

"We could always get pizza?"

What did that sound like to you? Was that exciting to read? No? Did it kind of make you want to bash your head against a wall? I hope so, because I wanted to smack my head against some form of inanimate object – hard – writing it.

This is an example of a conversation *you should not be having* with your respective other. While I won't say this isn't the sort of innocuous, indecisive chat you shouldn't have with anyone ever (although I'm thinking it), I will say that this sort of repartee is best left for in-person use only, lest you actually read back through said discussions and realize how utterly dry you sound. This isn't a relationship I'd want to be in. How about you?

Harsh? Maybe. But this is tough love, after all.

So, in addition to fun subjects like toenail picking, hair removal and the size of your latest BM, please avoid using email in the following situations:

To dump

Re: do NOT break up with someone over email unless it's a follow-up to the split. If you were too blindsided by the conversation to say everything you needed to say face-to-face, write it in an email. And then delete it, never to be read again.

As foreplay

You want to do what to his what? I'm sure he appreciates it, as will his friends if he decides to show said email around. His boss might enjoy it too, if it's been sent to his work account, but HR probably won't feel so turned on by your masterful tongue skills. If your boyfriend gets in trouble because of said email, he might not be as impressed with yours skills either – for that night, at least.

To have a standard, everyday conversation

I.E. the above, excruciatingly painful example.

Oh, don't complain. I know you've done those things (as do you) and though you can protest that they weren't 'so bad,' you're right. But do them more than a few times and you'll notice that the love affair you wish you were having suddenly seems a little tired, a little mundane. And who wants that?

So when *is* it acceptable to email your beloved?

When you're apart

Think of email as the modern-day version of snail mail. If he's on a business trip in the U.K. and you live in L.A., you'll have a nice little surprise waiting in your inbox when you wake up. If he's smart, it will say more than "Hey, how are you?" It will be a lengthy piece of prose about what he's been up to, how work is going, and how much he misses you.

If you've found something cute/funny/filthy that makes you think of him

Note: though writing erotica and sending it to his work account is a no-no, you can't be faulted for sending him an animated picture of Lois Lane telling Superman, "You're Superman, alright – in the sack" or something equally as cheesy/sexy – to his personal email account.

When it's practical

Does he need your grandmother's secret recipe for the lovely Spaghetti Bolognese he's going to attempt to make you? Does he need your flight details so he can pick you up at the airport? Email is, of course, the most common way to send said information, so utilize it.

CHAPTER 44:

WHY THE INFORMALITY OF EMAILING CAN CAUSE PROBLEMS

Whenever I receive a nasty email from someone, I always imagine myself actually confronting said offender and yelling, "Why don't you come out from behind your computer and say that to me? Grow a pair!" (Yes, even if it happens to be a girl.)

Although most situations don't warrant that kind of defiant response, (unless you're dealing with the dreaded breakup email, that is) the sentiment is still there. Why *don't* you leave your keyboard behind and say everything you wrote to my face? Oh wait, it's because you can't.

We feel freer to say the things we a) shouldn't b) can't or c) wouldn't dare under normal circumstances when there's distance between ourselves and our recipients. Sending something into the ether isn't as effective as seeing someone react to our words.

There are good things and bad things about emailing. Sending an electronic letter can be like a dose of truth serum, allowing us to say what we feel without feeling too vulnerable, but it can also be a quick an easy way to avoid a situation or cover up a lie.

Because we can't see the expression on the other's person's face or read their body language, it's often easy to misconstrue a situation or easily believe a fabricated story.

For example, perhaps the new guy you're dating sent you an email and said, "I'm so sorry I'm going to have to cancel on our date tonight. I'm feeling sick. Can we rain check? I'll make it up to you, I swear."

You can't see him: you have no way of knowing whether he's actually ill or not. But you want to believe him, so you do. In fact, you decide that he actually needs some TLC and bring homemade chicken soup to his house.

But he's not home...though he's sick. You're confused, and a little pissed off.

You get even more pissed off the next day when you check his Facebook wall and realize that he went out to watch a game with his guy friends. He *lied* to you – and you bought it, hook, line and sinker. Which makes him a stinker and you a sucker.

Or what about the time that you wrote a long, rambling email to the guy you had been out with four times when he simply asked you how your day was? Yes, you admit that two pages of prose about your evil boss might have been a little excessive, but you still can't understand why he didn't email you back…or call ever again.

Don't let informal emailing be your downfall, especially when it's so easy to avoid.

STEPHANIE'S STORY

"I exchanged email addresses with a guy I met during a work event one day. I'm big on networking, just as he appeared to be. Though we lived in completely different areas of California, we kept in touch.

"He lived in Long Beach, California, while I lived in San Francisco. When I happened to be back in the area for work again, we met up for lunch. We had a really good time and ended up spending the day together. Yes, we did kiss briefly – but it was such a small thing, and I felt absolutely no fireworks – so I really thought nothing of it. I mean, it was nice, but I wasn't thinking about it he next day. I liked him a lot though and thought of him as a very good friend. Our emailing became consistent and we eventually were chatting like we had known one another for years by exchanging text messages a few times a week and occasionally even calling one another on the phone.

"When I was back in his area yet again – to spend the holidays with friends, this time – he asked me to make a stop in Long Beach and spend the weekend with him. I couldn't see any reason why I shouldn't, so I did. Big mistake. It was the worst fail of a weekend of all time.

"It became all too apparent that he had been thinking of me as a potential girlfriend the entire time and that he thought that, because I decided to stay with him for the weekend, that he would treat me as such though we had only met a handful of times.

"I must have been seduced into thinking that I really knew him, that somehow we were closer than we actually were, over email. Everything was great and comfortable when I was hiding behind my computer screen, but when the reality of the situation hit me, it was just completely awkward. When I was with him, staying in his house and meeting his friends, it was real – and I didn't want to commit romantically to this person who had, for all intensive purposes, become my online pen pal.

"I'm not proud to admit this, but I had just moved to San Francisco and didn't know many people and was feeling a little lonely. I didn't have that many friends here yet and was missing my big network of male buddies. It was nice having a guy giving me attention and talking to me on a regular basis. For me, he was always just a pal. I wasn't attracted to him and yes, I guess I knew he liked me. But I realized after I kissed him that I could never look at him as a viable love interest, and that he could never become attractive to me in that way. He'll make a great boyfriend for someone though.

"In hindsight, it is possible that I led him on. I was more comfortable emailing him than seeing him in person, especially after I felt I realized he wanted a romantic relationship with me. I think because I felt pressure from him, I became standoffish and shy when I saw him in person.

"After I left his house that weekend, things were more than just a little off between us. He was offended by my attitude and confused by my lack of romantic interest. Needless to say, after that trip, he and I didn't talk anymore. I completely let the informality of emailing get to me and convinced myself that I was close to this person that I didn't know at all, apparently. But I'm not placing all the blame on myself, because he did the same by convincing himself that he was going to have a torrid love affair with a girl he had only ever met twice."

CHAPTER 45:

THE SNOOP

If I asked a room full of people to close their eyes and raise their hands if they had ever snooped through a partner's email, I bet no one would raise their hand. Why? The answer: because 99% of them *had* done so, and were too ashamed to admit it.

I have to say, though, that it's much easier to simply allow yourself to spy then to resist the temptation. It takes a very strong person to actively walk away from reading a respective other's email…especially if it's up and you're concerned about the state of your relationship.

Picture this: Your boyfriend has been acting weird, working late and you haven't had sex in ages. You suspect that he's cheating but have no way of proving your theory, and the anxiety is beginning to eat you up inside.

Flash to date night. He gets up to go to the restroom, leaving his Blackberry behind on the table. He'll be gone for three minutes, tops. But it's just lying there, and you need to know.

Do you resist, or do you read?

Let me tell you, the gal who read her boyfriend's email is going to be far worse off than the one who didn't.

"But I thought he was cheating – I needed to know!" you might protest. Lady, you doth protest too much. Not only are you automatically distrusting your guy, but you're actually causing more potential problems; busting open up Pandora's Box, if you will.

For argument's sake, let's say that your boyfriend was just stressed at work. However, in that brief time you had to snoop, you found a conversation between your boyfriend and one of his buddies saying that an ex had contacted him. He doesn't say much about that – it's just a mention – but that tiny piece of information is enough to send you into spasms of fear and insecurity.

Did reading his email set your mind at ease? No. Did it, in fact, cause you more grief? Sorry, but yes. Will it create problems in the future every time he stays out late or doesn't call right when he says he will? No doubt.

Searching through a partner's email isn't just bad for your emotional health, it's also illegal.

In 2008, an Oklahoma woman named Angel Lee learned this lesson the hard way.[42] She found

•••••••••••••••••••••••
42 *Wiehl, Lis.* March 6, 2008. <http://www.foxnews.com/story/0,2933,297859,00.html>.

327

herself in some scalding hot water after reading her husband's emails. Her spying started because she wanted to know what her husband and his ex were saying to one another, as they were going through a bitter custody battle. The judge in charge of the case sentenced her to sixty days of house arrest after deciding that she was in the wrong for using log-in information obtained without authorization.

How horrible – and harsh! But I bet it'll make you think twice before you reach for his Blackberry the next time he leaves it out around you, won't it?

ASHLEY'S STORY

"It was love at first site for me when I met Thomas. I had never felt that way about anyone before. We met on vacation, and I couldn't last a week without seeing him again. So I flew from the east coast to the west coast to see him immediately. I stayed for a few days, flew home and two weeks later I was back – and I stayed with him for months. It was an intense, passionate relationship.

"There was only one problem: he had recently come out of a ten-year relationship, and though there wasn't a prayer of he and his ex getting back together, I was still insecure about it. He clearly still thought about her and regretted her, though seemed to be getting over her with my help.

"For a while, my life was like a fairytale. We were constantly traveling together and he was always so romantic. I thought, 'If I love him this much, surely he's got to feel the same way?'

"One morning he needed to use my laptop to check his email, as he didn't have a computer at home. So he checked, kissed me goodbye and went off to work. When I finally got out of bed, I went to check my email and discovered that he was still logged in to his Gmail account.

"I knew it was wrong, but I couldn't resist. I got what was coming to me, though. To this day I still regret reading that email, and essentially blame my reading it for ruining our relationship.

"I mean, I *really* couldn't resist. A Gchat from his ex, Katie, was just open in front of me – and it was *about me*. I had to know what he was saying, what he thought about me – though I guess I should have just trusted him.

"Katie was writing about how pretty I was, and how happy she was that he had found someone who seemed to be so awesome. 'Is she your girlfriend?' was the last question she asked.

"His answer: 'She's just this girl I've been seeing.' I think my heart shattered into a tiny million little pieces. At that point, I had been basically living with him. We were together all the time. I thought of myself as his girlfriend. If I wasn't his girlfriend, what in the hell *was* I?

"When he came home from work that day, I was sullen and silent and resentful. My attitude had totally flipped, and my self-doubt began to cause problems. It was the beginning of the end for us, and all because I couldn't resist looking at his email.

"I should have realized that he wasn't going to immediately start gushing about me to a girl who not only dumped him and broke his heart, but started seeing someone else. Guys don't operate the same way that women do. But I didn't trust him – and I obviously shouldn't have trusted myself. His words hurt, but his actions at the time should have more than made up for that one measly little thing he said to her.

"But it didn't, and I lost him through my own insecurity. I should have known that sometimes *not* knowing is actually for the best. I do solemnly swear that I will never look through another boyfriend's emails, texts or Facebook messages ever again in my life. My snooping ruined my relationship and caused me to doubt myself for a very, very long time."

PART III:

FOURSQUARE

CHAPTER 46:

WHAT IS FOURSQUARE?

If you haven't heard of Foursquare, it's time to get with the program (and you call yourself a social media aficionado – the shame). Yes, it *is* a social networking site, as we've established, and one, that like the rest, that can be used for both good and evil.

Ostensibly, Foursquare is meant to help you make friends, discover cool and get discounts on things you like. Score! Who doesn't love a deal, after all?

On the other hand, Foursquare is also a site that that makes stalking – both the scary kind and the obsessive, "I want to see what he's up to" kind – possible.

There are currently 15 million users on the site, which launched in March 2009. That monster number of users check in on the site more than a billion times daily, which can equal a billion different types of trouble.

So how does it work? Well, you create a profile with a standard photograph, and when you get to your destination, you check in. You can be anywhere really, be it the doctor's office, home, a nightclub or a major event like the Oscars.

You also have the option of syncing up your account to your Facebook and Twitter pages; technically, all the world could know your whereabouts within a matter of seconds.

And of course, in addition to the aforementioned safety issues, there's unlimited potential here to cause a plethora of problems in an otherwise seemingly solid relationship.

CHAPTER 47:

WHEN YOU KNOW HE'S HIDING SOMETHING (LIKE HIS CHECK-INS)

In case you're still not quite getting the "point" of Foursquare, let me tell you this: it isn't *really* about making friends or meeting a mate. The site exists as a form of information sharing. Through user reviews you can determine what's hot and what's not. Plus, there's the incentive to check in and to become "The Mayor" of any spot you tend to frequent.

"The Mayor" may score some sweet deals. For example, if you head to your favorite bar and check in there every night for a week, eventually you'll take top dog status. While you're holding on to that title, the watering hole in question may be offering free rounds to the person who checks in the most – which just so happens to be you. You're going to do everything in your power to keep that title (free is your favorite flavor, after all), so you keep on returning night after night after night and drinking so much you're practically putting the place out of business.

Therefore, we should probably conclude that you *want* your check-ins to be seen, because you want to become the Mayor (otherwise known as the head honcho, top dog, conqueror and commander).

The more you start using Foursquare, the more obsessed you will become by it. It doesn't matter that you've become the mayor of your gynecologist's office, you're still the mayor, dammit! (So where in the heck is the 20% off that pap smear you were promised?)

So you and all of your friends are checking in like crazy, as is your boyfriend, who happens to be a big social media user. But one day – gasp! – he *hides his check-in* by "going off the grid." What does this mean, and is this a sign he's up to no good?

Sorry, but quite possibly. If he's still updating his Foursquare profile in the first place, he's not really "off the grid," as it were. He just doesn't want his location to be known – and that could be for a variety of nefarious to inconsequential.

He might be hiding his location because he's just discovered a rash in an unmentionable place and doesn't want you (or anyone else, really) to know that he's at his doctor's office. Why he chooses to update at all is a mystery, but then, Foursquare *is* addictive.

However, he could have hidden his check-in at a trendy restaurant – where's he gone with an attractive female co-worker that he has the hots for – so that you don't find out. He'll still get the credit on Foursquare, of course. Because that's important when you're about to be caught cheating...

But here's a trick for you, faithful readers. Going off the grid might hide his location, but it will still pinpoint his general location. For example, he thinks he's gone AWOL, but in fact his "off the grid" check-in places him somewhere in the general vicinity of the Upper West Side. You know that the only reason he would ever go that far uptown would be to see his ex-girlfriend; the one that came before you and broke his heart.

If you decided to get really crafty, you could pick a spot you knew he liked at random; if he had been there, his name would still show up on the venue's page. For example, say he and his ex went to Dive 75 for their first date and it was still a "special" spot for them both. If he as with her, you could go to Dive 75's Foursquare page and he, at least, would be checked in there.

Additionally, if you're constantly checked in to Foursquare on your Blackberry or Android, the applications on your phone might check you in without your knowledge thanks to your overworked GPS. This is just another way of saying "You're going to get *so* busted."

The only way of overturning this sly trick is to disable the location-based services on your phone. But he doesn't have to know that this option exists, right?

The moral of the story here is that you *can* see through his tricky ways – and he isn't as safe as he thinks he is if he's cheating and still using this particular form of social media.

ELLA'S STORY

"For the record, let me say that I love Foursquare. It's great on so many levels. It helps me work-wise (I work in PR) to do my expenses based on where I've been. It helps me remember places I've been that I liked, and it's also great when I'm bored. I can just look to see where my friends are and I'll automatically know where to go.

"On that note, you should know that I'm a big social media user. I'm always updating my Foursquare, Facebook and Twitter accounts. But I've had to curb my Foursquare use when I'm around my ex-boyfriend, Jeff, for one very important reason: his current girlfriend.

"I'm friends with all of my exes in a very nonsexual way, and Jeff is no different. We hang out all the time platonically. I did idly wonder if his current girlfriend, Katy, was against us hanging out, but I figured he would have said something if that was the case.

"I didn't find out until recently that she *does* have a problem with our friendship. He told me that he's started lying to his girlfriend whenever we hang out together because he knows it will upset her, and he won't let me tag him anymore on Foursquare.

"That may not sound like a big deal, but I check in *everywhere* on Foursquare, and I always say who I'm with. Like I said, I'm really big into using social media.

"I've honored his wishes, of course. They've been fighting a lot lately so he's trying to deflect further problems. Every time he brought up that we were hanging out, she'd get upset, so he's started lying to her and telling her he's working late. It's not right, but I get it. She's also on Foursquare, and checks his to see what he's up to. I don't want to cause additional problems by checking him into places, even though I'm not technically doing anything wrong."

CHAPTER 48:

WHEN TO LET HIM KNOW WHERE YOU ARE

You were a big Foursquare user at first. You were checking in left, right and center in the hopes of scoring some deals and/or becoming the mayor (you just like seeing your name next to a crown, it's empowering). But then your interest in the site tapered off thanks to your ADD, and you've started to use it for one thing and one thing only – to mess with your man's head.

For those of you who are thinking a sarcastic "Well, *that's* normal," I've got news for you: it actually is. Mature, no, but game playing is something we've all done and what most of us still do. There are just many more ways of figuring out your get-the-guy relationship strategy nowadays thanks to the Internet.

So what you've decided to do is a little role reversal, induce a little jealousy. You've decided that – because he doesn't know about that little location trick – you're going to ever so casually go off-the-grid at random times of the week, check in to places he'd never expect you to be and then *not mention them afterwards.* You are brilliant, or so you think.

Although a certain amount of cat and mouse is essential in any relationship – the guy does need to think you're a catch and not an easy, yet worthlessly attainable object, after all – creating ridiculous scenarios to make him jealous is *not* a good way to have an open and trusting relationship.

Sure, a little jealousy can be OK sometimes, but what if your little plan backfires? What if he actually thinks you're cheating on him, and then thinks, "Well two can play at this game!"

Conversely, he might not even notice the trickery you're employing. Men sometimes don't notice the obvious even when it's staring them straight in the face. Sorry, but he's probably *not* going to be stalking your Foursquare page in return.

My advice is this: check in as little or as much as you want to, as long as you're doing it because you want to. Don't create fake check-ins to make him jealous. Don't wish for a relationship based on lies.

On the other hand, if you happen to check in to a sex shop or his favorite bakery every once in a while – and I'm talking *very* infrequently – that could be a little exciting for him, especially if he's reaping the rewards of your little excursions later in the night.

CHAPTER 49:

HOW YOU CAN GET IN TROUBLE ON FOURSQUARE, AND HOW TO AVOID IT

Game-playing aside, the same rules apply for you as they do your respective other. You both have the ability to get in trouble, and you both have the ability to avoid said conflicts.

We've discussed how problems start, what he might be hiding from you and that he's clueless about the subtle tricks you're playing to make him jealous.

But when you beat a guy over the head with something obvious – like checking in to your ex-boyfriend's house or his place of work – your new guy *will* notice. This means: abort mission! But you knew that, right? *Right?*

Similarly, you don't want to be seen checking in to bars every night of the week or shouting, "OMG, just lost my bra in strip poker!" And if you think this should be totally obvious, that is correct – but some women still do so while inebriated.

Which brings me to how you can avoid getting yourself in trouble, be it with a boyfriend or with a guy who's interested enough to look at your Foursquare page. You shall weep with joy at the "delete" option.

Most people choose not to use this option, but then, those same people probably don't remember blearily checking in to their Foursquare account the night before in the first place. However, it does exist, so you might as well take advantage of it.

To erase your bad behavior, go to the Foursquare User History page and simply delete your old messages. It isn't rocket science and it *will* save your booty in the long run, so get on it.

CHAPTER TK:

BEWARE THE DANGERS OF FOURSQUARE

I really wish I could tell you that worrying about your boyfriend's whereabouts would be your biggest problem when using Foursquare but unfortunately, it's not. There are real dangers to using this site, and you should be aware of them.

Remember, when you're checking in somewhere, you're automatically letting people know exactly where you are, and that you're *not* at home.

First off, let's think smart. Foursquare, while a great social networking tool, is different from Facebook and Twitter in the sense that it's exclusively about placing yourself at different locations and perhaps even writing reviews about the spots you've been to. Because you're telling people exactly where you are, you should never, ever accept a friend request from someone you don't know well. Reserve this social networking site for people you know and trust.

Secondly, don't forget that Foursquare gives you the option of sharing your check-ins with your Facebook and Twitter followers. Facebook isn't a major problem, as most people don't tend to befriend strangers there, but Twitter is a different story. Unless you've locked your Twitter account – therefore negating the entire purpose of Twitter – your profile is open to everyone in the world. Which means that every time you check in on Foursquare and send it to Twitter, countless people you don't know could be watching your every move, including stalkers, online predators or rapists. Scary stuff indeed.

In addition to worrying about predators, you have to be wary of another sort of criminal: the robber. By constantly updating your Foursquare status, it's easy for thieves to know just when you're out of the house – and how much time they'll have to get their dirty work done. In 2011 a website was even launched to illustrate just how easy it is, in theory, to have all your worldly possessions taken while you were out gallivanting about town. Please Rob Me[43] exists to school you on what goes on while you're happily and ignorantly updating your various social networking statuses.

In conclusion here, again, just be smart. If you insist on checking in somewhere and sending it to Twitter, why don't you wait until you've actually

••••••••••••••••••••••••
43   <http://pleaserobme.com/>.

left the venue to announce that you've been somewhere cool? You'll still get your points, you'll still get closer to earning badges and a Mayorship, and you'll be that much safer.

On that note, please do not put a time stamp on your check-ins. With the ability to shout, or add a message to your status updates, it's all too easy to say, "Going to be at Café Cluny for the next two hours. Who's joining me?" You're literally begging for trouble.

TAYLOR'S STORY:
BEWARE THE CYBER STALKER

"A few years ago, I downloaded Foursquare to my iPhone. I'm not one to hook up with strangers, especially off of some app, but I was single and bored, and it was entertaining. For me, it was mostly a voyeuristic romp into the lives of Manhattan's most sexually adventurous individuals.

"One day I received a message from a guy who didn't have a profile picture. I must have been particularly bored that day, because I responded. He was reluctant to share any information and seemed overly nervous to reveal his true identity. Though this seemed weird to me, when he finally shared a few photos of himself, he was so stunning that I couldn't help but to continue chatting to him. At the very least, I thought I could meet him for a drink, though it was against everything I promised myself I'd be using the app for in the first place.

"I messaged him back and we carried on a conversation, which was cut short because he said he had a car waiting for him. Although he was complimentary, his tone was bratty and irreverent as he told me in no uncertain terms about the super exclusive, super chic-chic place he was going away to for the weekend. His arrogance, coupled with the fact that he was well spoken and clearly well educated only added to the intrigue.

"He began revealing small tidbits about his family. It was obvious that they were extremely wealthy -- and it was clear their wealth was of the old money variety. I'm a sucker for a bratty rich boy, so I acquiesced when he asked to exchange numbers.

"Over the week, I got an extremely detailed account of every move he made on his upper crust vacation, from mandatory cocktail hour with his stuck-up mother, to nights out on the town with his best friend and fights with his promiscuous older brother. The descriptions he gave were what I envisioned summers on the Kennedy's Martha's Vineyard compound to be.

"Soon he began dropping hints about the true identity of his family. He spoke of the companies his grandfather invested in, the celebrities he knew, leaning to swim at a Hollywood icon's home. It took me awhile, but with some proper investigating I finally found out who he was, and realized why he didn't want to be outed on Grindr.

"We had plans to meet up when he got back from his high-end family vacation, which began to sound more and more like something out of the *Great Gatsby*. He canceled, though, as he informed me that his grandmother had guilted him into going on yet another glamorous family excursion.

"I was fascinated by him, and found myself very much looking forward to getting his updates. He was interesting and intrinsically hilarious, but knowing his true identity gave me a real thrill.

"Our telephone and text messages increased. He began to send photographs of himself almost hourly. Our communication increased to such a degree that I realized I was developing a strange relationship with someone I had never even met. I was clicking with a stranger and being seduced into revealing intimate details about myself that I wouldn't normally confide.

"He finally told me that his grandmother was sending 'one of her planes' for him so he could fly back to the city and meet me. I was beyond excited. On the way, he informed me that he would be making a 'stopover' after his exotic vacation to visit his best friend from boarding school in Chicago.

"I was suspicious, so I asked him to document the trip through pictures. He happily complied. But then he told me that his best friend's father had passed away out of the blue, and I started to get angry. I knew there was always the chance that he was lying about who he was – he hadn't been completely honest with me from the get-go, after all – but it seemed like he was actually avoiding meeting me. I ultimately decided I needed to know the truth, so I demanded that he tell me who he really was.

"This perfect guy, this heir to one of New York's most famous families, was actually a portly, 30-something guy from the Midwest who happened to see me walk into my Midtown office building one day and developed a 'thing' for me. He went on Grindr and thought he had 'scored' when he found me, calling me 'the perfect specimen.' He admitted to standing on the corner and waiting for me to leave my office more than a few times. He would watch and wait. He said that he thought he could never have me, but wanted to experience what it was like to get close to someone so 'perfectly beautiful.'

"Obviously this situation made me sick. I though the best course of action was to just disappear and not aggravate him, but I still wonder if he's still there, watching. I've learned my lesson and refuse to mess with Foursquare or other similar sites that lets strangers know my whereabouts."

PART IV:

MYSPACE

CHAPTER 50:

YES, MYSPACE STILL EXISTS

I refuse to think that I'm aging myself by remembering when MySpace was cool, given that it only started hitting its glory days in 2005. But the site now seems like a dinosaur in lieu of all the new social networking services floating around the Internet. And by dinosaur, I mean a relic. A fossil. Something old, and so on and so forth.

In its heyday – 2005 until early 2008 – MySpace was the most visited social networking site in the world. Halfway through 2006 it even surpassed Google as the most visited website in the United States. At its peak in 2008, the site attracted 75.9 million monthly unique visitors and was valued at a staggering $12 billion.

But nothing lasts forever, right? The website saw a major decline as competing sites like Facebook started to crop up on the world wide web. MySpace, which was primarily used to find like-minded people interested in entertainment, music and pop culture, couldn't find its footing in the new social networking subculture and users started to lose interest. I personally haven't used the site since early 2009, and I'm not alone: over the past two years, MySpace has lost, on average, more than a million U.S. users a month.[44] From June 2009 to June 2011, its staff was reduced from 1,600[45] to 200 employees.[46] You see where I'm going with this…the site was in trouble.

It used to be a place where music lovers could unite, and you could meet a guy because you both really dug Eminem, or The Killers, or were even both closet *American Idol* fans. And although the site was on 24/7 Wall Street's annual list of brands that would disappear in 2012[47], there's hope for the once hot, now not website yet.

That great white hope, as it were, is none other than former 'N Sync singer Justin Timberlake, who bought the site for a measly $35 million in mid-2011[48] (remember, the site was once worth *$12 billion*).

•••••••••••••••••••••••••••
44 *Gillette, Felix.* June 22 2011. <http://www.businessweek.com/magazine/content/11_27/b4235053917570.htm>.

45 *Arrington, Michael.* June 16 2009. <http://techcrunch.com/2009/06/16/myspace-executes-30-staff-reduction-today/>.

46 *Vascellaro, Jessica E.* June 30, 2011. <http://online.wsj.com/article/SB10001424052702304584004576415932273770852.html>.

47 *McIntyre, Douglas A.* June 22, 2011. <http://247wallst.com/2011/06/22/247-wall-st-ten-brands-that-will-disappear-in-2012/4/>.

48 *Fixmer, Andy.* June 29, 2011. <http://www.businessweek.com/news/2011-06-29/news-corp-calls-quits-on-myspace-with-specific-media-sale.html>.

Although it's not currently a dating hotspot, there's no doubt that the gorgeous singer is going to infuse some sexy back into MySpace. In fact, he's already started, announcing a partnership between his new company and electronics giant Panasonic in January 2012. [49]

The joint venture will be called MySpace TV and incorporates the social media element that the site has lacked in recent years. It's meant to allow users to talk about and share the shows they're watching as well as to invite friends to watch with them. The music component the site was previously known for is still there too: the network's library has 100,000 music videos and 42 million songs.

But will MySpace become a relevant place to look for love, as it was before? That still remains to be seen.

At the height of its popularity though, many users were heading to MySpace to perk up their love lives and to score dates through the site. Strange? Not really, given that MySpace was to the early 21st century what Facebook is to the world today.

49 *Ngak, Chenda.* January 10 2012. <http://www.cbsnews.com/8301-501465_162-57356311-501465/justin-timberlake-announces-myspacetv-at-ces-2012/>.

RONNIE'S STORY:
RECONNECTING THROUGH MYSPACE

"Reggie and I went to the same high school until I moved from California to Connecticut during my junior year. We didn't know one another, but we knew *of* one another. I knew what truck he drove and the he played water polo. He knew that I owned an orange super Beetle. We were at the same parties and in the same group, but just didn't know one another.

"Ten years later, I was living in New York City and about to move back to California. I was home one night and bored, so started playing on MySpace when I found him under my high school's alumni page. I thought to myself, 'Hm, I think I knew of him and he got cute,' so I sent him a MySpace message as well as a friend request. He got replied right away and said that he had recently moved back to San Francisco, which was where I was heading, too. He asked if I wanted to meet up when I moved back to the area.

"I definitely wanted to, but in that two months before I headed west, we got to know one another really well over MySpace. We talked so much that we learned a lot about one another without actually meeting face to face. Literally two weeks after I moved back, we met up for the first time (ever) and started dating almost immediately. We got married last fall. Christmas day we go to his parents' house, who just so happen to live right around the corner from my parents. It's perfect; it was meant to be.

"I always think, none of this would have happened if not for MySpace. It was the tool that allowed us to meet back up, the catalyst that brought us together. MySpace at its peak was what Facebook is today. It was a way for me to connect with someone I wouldn't have met otherwise, and I'm eternally grateful for it."

RENAE'S STORY:
MEETING A STRANGER
THROUGH MYSPACE

"I met my husband by a fluke. A high school friend got me to join MySpace because of my upcoming high school reunion. So I joined, and my only online friends were from my graduating class. I was single at the time and didn't plan on meeting anyone online, but then Frank asked me to be his friend.

"I was very reluctant to do so, but I said yes anyway. Why not? So we talked online for about three weeks until he eventually gave me his phone number. I didn't call him though. After six weeks of talking online, I finally gave him my number and he called me right away.

"It wasn't too long after we had been chatting on the phone that we met in person; about a week. I was still skeptical about meeting someone in person that I had met online though, so we talked on the phone for about five hours each night until we met.

"I knew that I liked him a lot, and I didn't have feelings right away when we were talking online. But when we met in person, I knew it: he was the one. I had butterflies in my stomach.

"We started dating immediately and he proposed six months later. We got married in May of 2009."

PART V:

CUPIDRADAR

CHAPTER 51:

THE WAVE OF THE FUTURE

I thought I'd finish this book talking about an innovative new app that might just get the computer obsessed out from behind their safe screens and interacting in society. If we're operating behind the premise that there's different strokes for different folks, then CupidRadar rubs me the right way (so to speak).

While some people prefer to take their time getting to know someone online, there are others that believe it's a waste to spend hours talking, talking, talking only to find they have zero chemistry in person.

CupidRadar founder and CEO Mehrdad Sarlak is one of those people. He believes that we need to create our own destiny, that our soulmate might be living in the house next door and we'd never know it, because we don't know *them*.

That's why he developed a safe, innovative Smartphone app that allows you to meet the potential stranger of your dreams. The company's slogan says it all: "While destiny brings you close, CupidRadar brings you closer."

Here's all you need to know in order to put Cupid on *your* radar...

What is it?

CupidRadar is a Smartphone app that allows you to safely meet other singles in your area.

How does it work?

The site uses a GPS-like tracking device to tell you when similar-minded singletons are nearby. You can then message those that you might be interested in and ask them to meet up.

How to start

You'll create a painless free profile with a headline, About Me section and basic information like your height and age. You'll then add a photograph or two and download the app to your Smartphone.

Is it safe?

Very. Your profile has to be approved by the CupidRadar team before you're even allowed to start using the app. They site also keeps a vigilant watch on those who might be sending out red flags. According to Sarlak, no one is allowed to change their gender, date of birth or create various profiles with similar email addresses. Those who attempt to sign up without a legitimate profile picture won't be approved and people lying about their sign-in location with be blocked.

Although CupidRadar will tell you if another single is nearby, your exact location is never pinpointed. The app will still tell you you're a mile away from a potential love interest even if they're standing right next to you in order to avoid a stalker-like situation. It will also round to the nearest mile: if you're 2.95 miles away, your location will be rounded up to 3 miles.

If you want no part of the guy that's been messaging you from Rodeo Drive (he's old enough to be your dad!) you can click a 'Not interested' button, and Sugar Daddy will be gone from your life forever. Similarly, if you've exchanged somewhat personal details with someone and don't want evidence of the things you've shared, the worrisome messages will disappear along with your interest. You can still remain completely anonymous.

You will also never have to give your phone number or email address to a stranger: you can message exclusively through the site.

I love the idea that our destiny could be passing us by and it is only by communicating *in person*, by stepping outside of our comfort zone, that we might meet our potential soulmate.

Are there any hidden fees?

It's free to sign up, but each connection you make is $2. That means you'll pay $2 for unlimited contact with a certain person/interest and you can communicate without ever having to give the other your personal details.

Who uses this app?

The typical user ranges from his/her early 20's to late 30's, though there is a handful of people in their late 50's and early 60's using the site. Most are educated and the male/female ratio is split nearly down the middle with slightly more men at 55/45.

Where does the app work?

The technology works worldwide, but the company is currently focusing on marketing in the USA. It has been tested for use in Europe, China and the Middle East as well.

How will I know if I have anything in common with the singles in my area?

The app offers a service called Cupid Concierge, where you can set your radial distance of interest and how often you want to be notified when someone in the area fits your criteria. Even better, it's free.

AN INTERVIEW WITH CUPIDRADAR CEO & PRESIDENT MEHRDAD SARLAK

"I've always been fascinated with why people who choose certain people and why they mate with who they mate. I also don't think it's fair that it's so easy to tell who's married but there's absolutely no way to tell who's single. I thought, 'How can I use technology to see who's single and help people come together?' Thus, the idea for CupidRadar was born.

"I'm trying to use technology as a lever to bring people together in a semi-old fashioned way, like our parents used to. Before online dating, Facebook and Twitter, you'd meet someone at a gas station, or a park, or the grocery store. When you met someone for the first time, you didn't know anything about him or her. You didn't know how much money they made, or their level of education. You had to actually speak to them in person to learn anything about them. Nowadays, you can access someone's personal information with the click of a button. There's no mystery. Education and communication is a lost art.

"In terms of being a matchmaker, I'm very much someone who believes in individual integrity. It offends my intellectual sensibilities that the competitive sites – eHarmony, Chemistry, Match – attempt to do the thinking for you. I've used every dating site that there is and have repeatedly taken the overly long psychological tests. I've found the results of their mathematical algorithms to be absurd. I don't drink or use drugs, but I've been matched with drunks in the past.

"Then, once you've joined these sites, you send out hundreds of emails to people because you feel obligated to get your money's worth. Of that number, one or two people will actually respond to you. When you eventually connect with this person, what ensues is a long, drawn-out process where you have a phone, email and text relationship. That's just not natural; that's not how we're meant to have evolved.

"After communicating purely by these methods, you've wasted up to a month with a person you haven't even met yet. Despite all the time you've taken getting to know the other, within a minute and a half of meeting him or her, you'll know whether or not you feel any chemistry or are attracted to them. You'll know if she or he is or isn't the one. It's such a waste of time. You might think to yourself, 'If only I had met this person on day one, I wouldn't have wasted the last few weeks getting to know someone that ultimately isn't right for me. I don't think this way of inverting relationship beginnings is natural.

"CupidRadar's technology lets you know on a basic level who's single around you. I'm not telling you who to be with. I'm not Cupid. If you work, you work. If you don't, you don't. It's your prerogative.

"Do you ever stop to think about the people that pass you by on a daily basis? Do you think that someone you may never meet is the person for you? We're operating under the premise that, though destiny got you close, we're physically bringing you together."

CHAPTER 52:

SUMMING IT UP

It's sad but true that your love life may not flourish during this time of TMI. In fact, aside from a few isolated incidents, it appears that Twitter, emailing and Foursquare can do your relationship more harm than good. Remember to:

♥ Never befriend someone you don't know on Foursquare

♥ Send your Foursquare check-ins to Twitter

♥ Don't play games using social media – they'll cause more problems for your relationship and/or be ignored entirely

♥ Avoid saying anything you wouldn't want shared on email

CHALLENGE: Why don't you take your love life entirely off-line for a while? Communicating in person isn't *so* awful, is it? And if you're scared the other person might bite, well, that *could* be construed as a good thing.

CHAPTER 53:

IN CONCLUSION

So, OK, online dating and navigating the wily world of social media isn't actually *You've Got Mail*. There isn't always a happy ending, and the guy you're talking to probably isn't going to be as nice as Tom Hanks. It can be difficult, you have to be cautious and you'll have to walk a fine line between revealing too much and revealing too little.

That said, what do you have to lose by refusing to at least try online dating? It's a great way to people if you're busy or you're shy or new to an area. It is the second most common way to meet people these days, so I really think it's time you dropped your prejudices and got over the stigma that meeting someone online is cheesy or uncool. It's not, but you will be for being so closed-minded.

Matchmaking sites like Match and Chemistry, as well as social media sites like Facebook and Twitter have given us the ability to connect with people we wouldn't have met otherwise, but at some point, we have to remember that romantic relationships are meant to be personal. All of the above are great tools that should be implemented and taken advantage of, but they shouldn't be used in lieu of having a real relationship. We have to exist with someone in reality, and *not* just in a virtual world.

I don't want to have an email-only relationship, or a month of endless messages without a date in sight on Match.com. As much as I love Facebook, I don't need a status to define my relationship, nor do I need my 1,700 "friends" to know about it when I *do* decide to give it a title.

I especially don't need to see what an ex is getting up to – and I don't have to, anymore. With one quick click of the 'unsubscribe' button and a lot of willpower, I kicked my addiction. In the end, it wasn't such a hard habit to break.

On that note, my advice to you is this: do yourself a favor and refrain from all that 'It's complicated' malarkey, because really, 'it' doesn't have to be. When love is right, it's right...regardless of where you find it.

APPENDIX

LOVE BY THE NUMBERS

Are you ready to break it down? These statistics show online love by the numbers --- and yes, you *will* be quizzed afterwards.

140 million – The number of online daters in China

87 million – The number of single people in the United States

40 million – The number[50] of single online daters in the United States

20 million – The number of people using eHarmony

120,000 – The number of marriages per year that result from Internet matches

1,400 – The number of online dating sites that exist today

50 *Fox News*. February 7, 2012. <http://www.foxnews.com/scitech/2012/02/07/in-modern-valentine-quest-dating-is-digital/>.

100 – The number of miles most people are willing to travel for love

20 – The percentage online dating memberships increased in 2012

5 – The number of guys you should be talking to (but not going on serious dates with) at once when initially entering the online dating world

5 – A good number of photos to post so that you don't look a) too egocentric or b) that you are not actually who you claim to be

4 – The number of billions the online dating industry is now worth worldwide.

3 – The amount of weeks you should wait before meeting in person. If he hasn't asked you out or professed a desire to after two weeks of chatting, it's a probable guarantee that he isn't going to.

1 – At the end of the day, the number of matches you really need to work out.

0 – The number of times you should contact a guy first

Also From New Chapter Press

TITANIC: THE TENNIS STORY
-by Lindsay Gibbs

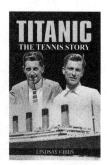

In a love story that rivals that of the fictional account of Jack and Rose from the blockbuster movie TITANIC, this is a narrative of an incredible real-life story of triumph, survival and romance. The book tells the tale of American tennis star Karl Behr and the pursuit of the love of his life, Helen Newsom, and how they both survived the sinking of the famous ship and how Karl crossed paths with future U.S. champion Dick Williams aboard the rescue ship *Carpathia*. Two years after the tragedy, the two become teammates on the U.S. Davis Cup team and meet in the quarterfinal round of the modern day US Open.

ACING DEPRESSION:
A TENNIS CHAMPION'S TOUGHEST MATCH
-by Cliff Richey

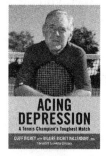

Chronicling the tumultuous life of the original "bad boy" of tennis, this engaging and inspirational memoir describes one man's public battle with clinical depression. Cliff Richey was best known for the 1970 season in which he was the No. 1 U.S. tennis player who reached the semifinals of the French and US Opens and helped lead the U.S. to victory at the Davis Cup. Documenting his 10-year fight for control of his mind, aided by antidepressant medication, the determination and strength that afforded him the nickname of "The Bull" is highlighted. Expressing the joy of feeling stable for the first time in his life, this deeply moving story of nightmare and redemption serves to encourage and inspire anyone whose life is touched by mental illness.